INNER FREEDOM

ALSO BY KEITH MERRON, Ed.D:

~ The Golden Flame: The Heart and Soul
   of Remarkable Leadership

~ Consulting Mastery: How the Best Make the
   Biggest Difference

~ Riding the Wave: Designing Your Organization's
   Architecture/or Enduring Success

INNER FREEDOM

Living Authentically
the Life You Were Truly Meant to Live

A Practical Guide to Fulfillment

By Keith Merron, Ed.D.

Integral Publishers
1418 N. Jefferson Ave.
Tucson, AZ 85712

Cover art by Jeannie Carlisle

Poems by David Whyte used with permission.
Poem by Javan from *Something to Someone*, Jacan Press 1984.

Printed in the United States, the United Kingdom and Australia to minimize shipping distances and reduce the negative impact on our environment. Lightning Source has the following environmental printer Chain of Custody certifications: Forest Stewardship Council™, Sustainable Forestry Initiative®, Programme for the Endorsement of Forest Certification™.

ISBN 978-0-9892220-0-6

Dedication

My father, above all, followed the beat of his own drum and as a result, taught me the greatest lesson in life, to be my own person. It is in his honor that this book is dedicated.

CONTENTS

ACKNOWLEDGEMENTS

No man is an island and a book never written without support and inspiration from others. Over the years I have been deeply moved and influenced by some extraordinary mentors and teachers, each of whom have challenged me toward my greatest self. Included among them are Bill Torbert, Michael McKeon, Martha Borst, David Bradford and Mayuri Onerheim to whom I am deeply indebted.

Many friends and colleagues have been models of authenticity and embodiment and they have been enormous support to me as I walk life's path. By their conduct and character, I have been moved. Among them are Deborah Wilder, Marty Kaplan, Bill Stevens, Katharine Boshkoff, Mark Voorsanger, Steve Tennant, Tina Benson, Tim Kelley, Lion Goodman, Barbara Annis, and David Wilcox.

Larry Boggs, my editor, did an outstanding job in raising the precision of my writing as well as gifting me with thoughts that have meaningful enhanced the quality of expression.

This book could not have been written except for the lessons of my parents who, by the way they lived their life, taught me to thy own self be true.

LETTER TO MY SON

Dear Josh:

As you near the end of your college life and begin to prepare yourself for life in the world, I'd like to share some thoughts with you. There are countless expectations placed on us from everywhere concerning how to perform, how to succeed, how to become a man of honor and love. As I come into the middle years of my life, I can finally see that many parts of my life were scripted for me, following the archetypal patterns that so many men fall into. We know those archetypes all too well—being a heroic provider and equating success with economic achievement or peer recognition top the list. These goals may result in congratulations but can leave a scar in one's heart. We can become so busy attaining something out there that we fail to see or follow the calling of our hearts. I have followed unconsciously some of the powerfully etched expectations of my father, his father, and fathers before them, and more recently I've wondered about how these expectations have affected me and our culture as a whole. Sadly, I could not clearly see how much of a hold these expectations had on me as they began to form and take over early on in life. These false ideals have saturated our society, family, and community to such an extent that it doesn't occur to us to step out of our assigned roles and see them for what they are.

And so, without my knowing it, I have done the same in kind; I have tried to shape you and mold you to be the man I imagined you should be, and I did this unconsciously, unaware of how my own efforts were designed to fill a hole in my own life. For some reason, we fathers seem naturally suited to being torchbearers for our children—except that what we are passing on to the next generation is not wisdom from our hearts and souls, but our own sense of loss and fear, and our own lock-step conformity to certain expectations. We tell you how to lead a good life and give you things and experiences in the hope that you form into the shape of our desires (or what we think are our desires) rather than the shape of yours.

I at last see that while I may have tried to convince myself that I wanted the best for you, the deeper truth is that I wanted what I thought was the best for me. The problem is that the best for me may not at all be the best for you. So as I begin to fully and finally embrace the man I was meant to me, I realize that each must travel their own path and make their own discoveries. An inkling of this awareness came to me years ago when I learned that my success strategy of working extremely hard and trying to get ahead in life had the wonderful result of good solid earnings, but the sad result of not being able to stop and smell the roses and enjoy the sweet nectar that life offers us in each moment. So committed was I to bettering myself that I failed to discover and appreciate what I truly am—and failed to see that being what I am is good enough.

For whatever reason, you have been able to hold yourself as "good enough" just as you are, and so you have appeared "not driven" to me. Since my own success strategy has been to strive and work hard, I've feared that you would not succeed, given your inclinations. What I failed to recognize is that success comes in many forms, and my success strategy need not be yours. Trying to get you to follow my strategy was a flawed one, and perhaps even damaging. Given what a strong and emotionally solid man you seem to be becoming, I am comforted in knowing the damage is reparable.

We laughed a few years ago about how your biorhythms are similar to those of Zen masters. Now I see that there is more to that than I had realized. You have been a teacher for me, and one thing you have taught me is that I have much to learn about relaxing and simply being, with no agenda and no place to go. To the extent that I can now see you embodying a quality I have disowned for so many years, you are a grand teacher indeed.

Josh, the book I am sharing with you is my ode to an authentic life. It was written as both a guidebook and as a philosophy, one that I now embrace with all my being. Please forgive me for the years that I lived in the illusion that my job was to mold you, and know that you are an extraordinary young man, just as you are. Your beauty is beyond compare to me, and I relish the moment you were born and cherish the life you have forged for yourself. If there is one gift I could give, one that may be more important than any other, it is to honor you, just as you are.

This book is my gift to you, the writing of which has taught me much, and the sharing of which gives me great pleasure. May it support you in whatever ways it was meant to support you, and know that I love you with all my heart and soul.

With Gratitude and love,
Dad

INTRODUCTION

"I would rather be ashes than dust! I would rather that my spark should burn out in a brilliant blaze than it should be stifled by dry rot. I would rather be a superb meteor, every atom of me in magnificent glow, than a sleepy and permanent planet. The proper function of man is to live, not to exist. I shall not waste my days in trying to prolong them. I shall use my time."

– Jack London

One of our greatest fears is loss of control. This fear is nearly universal, whether it involves the dread of losing our overall sense of self and our perceived role in life, or anxieties regarding some specific area—health, money, relationships, work, or sense of meaning. As a result, we try to hold on to all that we have—including the "life script" that we think is ours. Even in the face of enormous evidence that our lives are not working, and that the script itself is leading to an undesired outcome, we hold on tight, hoping that with a little more effort or luck things will turn around for us. For most of us, the life-script that we find ourselves enacting was not something we chose. Instead, it was given to us over time by the multitude of messages we received from our parents, our teachers and schoolmates, from government and business leaders, and from advertisements and through the media in general. This process began well before our earliest life memories and has been continually reinforced by society—and internalized by us—to this day. Deeply as we are wedded to our life narrative, for so many of us, it is not in any real sense our "own." It is assigned to us by others and consciously or unconsciously adopted by us. Like someone else's coat, we wear it, but too often it does not fit the shape of who we really are.

It is no wonder that the adopted role we wear is not only a poor fit; it actually hides us from ourselves. It keeps us from discovering and fulfilling our deeper life purpose, and from finding our deeper joy. The good news is that once we understand this false identity that we are living, we begin to loosen its shackles in every area of our lives and discover a passion, enjoyment, and sense of purpose that we may not have imagined was possible.

Coming to that realization is not easy; for many people it is a life's work. From a very young age we were told by parents, teachers, peers, and the mass media how to live and behave, who we are, what we should aspire to be, and what we must avoid. For most of us, our life scripts have offered us a false identity that got attached to us through our early associations, and this identity has become self-reinforcing throughout our lives.

We may or may not perceive our estrangement from our true self, but one can slowly die of starvation—in body or soul—without realizing it. Whether we know it or not, nearly all of us are, to one degree or another, fundamentally depressed and unfulfilled at the core of our being. Some of us are aware of that fact but feel helpless to change it, and others of us are relatively unaware if it. Either way, we resort to "fixes" that may temporarily reduce our level of discomfort but do nothing to address the core problem. Alcohol, narcotics, and many pharmaceutical drugs are used for this purpose—but so are sex and relationships, simplistic belief systems or "answers" about life, therapies of every sort, sports (whether as participant or spectator), activism of all kinds, and being immersed in work (often to the detriment of our loved ones). All of these things are used as distractions from the underlying pain of separation from our core self and values. The deeper disturbances remain because we are still living a false script. Unfortunately, we have worn the wrong coat for so long that it appears more comfortable than the one that is truly our own. It offers us enough of something—warmth, security, material possessions, and the like—that we see it as better than the uncertainty we'd have to face in taking it off and finding and wearing the one that fits our true self.

I have a friend who a short time ago was on the brink of suicide because his false identity came crashing down around him. The story is all too familiar. For years he had an increasing sense of anxiety, depression, and hopelessness. For well over 20 years my friend struggled with his business, attempting to build it up to the point where he could sell it and reap the financial benefits of his efforts for himself and his family. Along the way he borrowed well over $1 million from family and friends to fuel the dream. Recently, mired in debt, he had to close his business and declare bankruptcy. He sold his house at a time when the housing market was taking a nosedive to he could pay back his remaining assets to some of his investors.

He had to start again from zero. For over a year he has been looking for a job but unable to find one; he is overqualified for almost every job available. After 20 years of chasing the American Dream, and discovering it to be more distant and elusive than ever, he felt defeated and hopeless. He called me to tell me he was feeling suicidal.

To his friends, this man appears hugely talented, wise, loving, kind, playful, and filled with integrity. Something of his true self still radiates through his being. The problem is simple: Like so many of us, this beautiful man has always been living the script that molded his outlook from infancy and has since reinforced itself through repetition and interaction with others, who help perpetuate the illusion. The American Dream of material success became his own dream, or so he thought—and when that dream crashed, he believed the wreckage of the dream contained his very soul. He seems to have failed in that to which he gave his all. But the problem is not in this "failure," but in his attachment to the dream, with no other place to locate his sense of self.

My friend is far from alone. Billions of people suffer from the same malady, even if their exact circumstances and ways of dealing with them are not the same. We have glimpses of how we would like to feel. We occasionally let down our guard and allow a sense of primal joy or even sublimity to leak through—as when we have fallen in love, or are enjoying moments of intimacy, or are immersed in the beauties of nature, or even experience moments of "reality shifts" (spontaneously or through assisted means) where everything seems transcendent and glowing. Other kinds of moments are also "designed" to achieve this state—from sporting events and competitions to movies and artistic performances. But these glimpses of primal joy are temporary, and when they are gone, we can actually suffer a sense of loss—as well as the apparent inability to re-achieve that state at will. And then only the preprogrammed drone of our lives remains; and more often than not, our "happiness"—like that of my friend—seems to be tied up in how well our script is succeeding or failing.

Our scripts, our values, and our beliefs about ourselves come from our surroundings. One cannot really change this script without first recognizing at a very personal level where it came from (and continues to come from) and why there are so many internal and external pressures to conform to it. In this book we shall delve into these issues in depth. One thing worth pointing out here, though, is that this description applies to everyone. There are no "masterminds" controlling us; in other words, there's really no "us versus them" involved here. In a sense, everyone is both "victim" and "perpetrator" (or at least appears to take on these roles). We create the scripts for others, just as others create our scripts, and most of the time we are unaware of our role in this, just as we are unaware of the extent to which our culture has molded us. In any case, there is no blame—just the need to understand and grow beyond our situation.

If the studies of many archaeologists are correct, we can be quite certain that the scripts and false identities that bedevil us today, though seemingly everywhere, are not a constant of the human experience. Prior to the transition from hunting/gathering cultures to agrarian economies, humans lived in a cocoon of community, with all the cooperation and support that entails. Survival was a daily reality, no different from today, but a greater sense of simplicity, natural collaboration, and magical joy was likely a given as well.

The disturbing tension between individuality and collective effort, which is so much a part of the scripts that we live, is a modern distinction, born out of politics and strife. When humans were hunters and gatherers, self and community were intermingled—almost one and the same. In fact, the concept of "self" in the sense that we think of it did not exist. When we gave, we gave freely to others, for they were a part of us. Connection was woven into the fabric of reality itself; it wasn't something anyone had to think about. Similarly, authentic expression was natural, for there was no environment for inauthenticity to thrive.[1] But now, more than ever, our culture "writes" the unwritten rules for behavior. Today's choice is a simple one, a choice our hunter and gatherer ancestors never faced. It is the choice of either living in a way our culture dictates for us—a set of dictates that we have internalized, largely to our detriment—or to live authentically, expressing who we are at the deepest level, a level that most of us have yet to discover. The ego with which we identify today is not our deepest identity but an artificial construct. It came into existence with the advent of the agrarian, domesticated economy and the competition and societal rules that resulted. The ego identifies with our given script rather than with our deeper, authentic purpose.

It is the intention of this book to inspire you and provide you with tools to let go of the "ego" construct and instead follow the inner magic that lies deep within you. The book is part of the larger dance of life as we seek to individuate and embody our true selves. It is dedicated to helping you loosen the ego's shackles and thus reclaim the deep passion and higher purpose that lie within you. Then you will be inspired to forge ahead in the creation of a life that is uniquely and authentically your own.

HOW TO USE THIS BOOK

There are two primary types of books on the market today. One type is source material; intended to be read and digested. We often read these books passively. The other type is a workbook, where the author is guiding you in a process of learning. We often engage in these books actively. This book is a hybrid. The source material is intended to offer a perspective and the exercises are designed to invite you to engage fully with the source material, and more importantly, with your life.

This book is best read with a journal by your side. Whenever a thought or a discovery occurs, write it down in your journal. Allow yourself to write spontaneously as discoveries occur along the way. These discoveries may occur as you read, or they may occur in the context of living your life. When they do, jot them down in your journal to allow you to track your unfolding discoveries.

In each chapter, you will be invited to engage in exercises. Follow the exercises offered in each chapter or adapt them to your liking. Readers who have benefitted most from the book and its exercises typically do most exercises as written, and then adapt some to fit their own sense of what will challenge them most at this moment in their life. If you do choose to adapt an exercise, be sure to keep to its spirit and essence.

When there is an exercise or a particularly valuable moment to write in your journal, we will note it clearly with the following symbol:

This is an indication that it is time to pause, reflect and write those reflections down. In this way, the book becomes a teaching, a guide, and a call to your own inner discoveries.

Here is your first exercise of many.

Your First Exercise

A life script is a script by which you have lived your life. It is typically an unconscious script that has shaped your life. Imagine your life as a Greek tragedy, filled with all kinds of characters: villains, buffoons, heroes, and a powerful story line where the possibility of a great life was thwarted by society, family, community, a person, or any of a number of forces. It is a sad story, or perhaps a hopeful story, but filled with untapped potential.

Get in touch with the ache in your soul, that part of you that knows you are not living fully the life you were meant to live. Feel the frustration, the thwarted efforts, the yearnings, and the misfortunes. See the choices you've made that played a part in the current sense of not being fully fulfilled.

Now write the story that feels most true to where you are now. Begin the story like this:

"There once was a boy/girl born into a (describe the world he/she was born into). He/she came into the world with enormous potential and promise. He/she had something extraordinary to bring to the world. He/she was a gift. But alas, the world was not ready, or seemed to have different plans . . . "

Or begin it in your own way. Allow it to unfold without you getting into your head too much. This is not a practice in imagination or creativity. It is a practice in listening to and honoring the truth of what your life has been. Listen with your body. Listen to what your intuition knows is true about where you are at this point in your life.

CHAPTER ONE

A HIDDEN WHOLENESS

*"When physical vision has transcended space,
another sky opens to the eyes of the soul."*

–Rumi

This book is a story of our lives. It is not the only way of perceiving our lives. It is just one perspective, but it is an important one with crucial implications. It is about a dimension of our lives that is native and natural to us, and yet it has been largely obliterated from our awareness—perhaps contained only as a vestige of childhood memory. Thomas Merton, famous for his writing about the inner world, often described life as if it had contained within it a natural and pure shape. He often spoke of it as a hidden wholeness. He was referring to the shape that our lives are designed to discover. And so often we fail to live that life. It eludes us, for it is so difficult to see—and even more difficult to honor and follow. As a result, we lead frustrating and unfulfilling lives. When we do take on the shape of what we were meant to be, we feel extraordinary inner freedom.

In three decades of consulting to and writing about leadership, as well as delivering hundreds of workshops to help people find their most powerful hidden wholeness, I have discovered that if this perspective is fully taken in, it becomes a very powerful shape-shifter that can utterly transform our outlook, enhance our creativity, and help us discover our own unique purpose.

If this perspective is so much a part of us, why is it hidden from our view? Much of the answer to this question has to do with how we view the world and ourselves. Our view, far from being our conscious creation, was, in effect, "downloaded" into us by parents, teachers, peers, and larger cultural influences without our knowledge or consent, and has ever since resulted in a case of our own "mistaken identity." In a very real sense, most of us do not know who we are.

What are these cultural influences that prevent us from knowing ourselves? Primary among them is the western model of medicine and psychology that our modern world has taken on. Far from being of purely academic interest, this model forms the fabric of our culture itself. This model assesses and judges our own mental and emotional health on the basis of how well we've adapted to the expectations of our culture. Using this model, a healthy person is a "well-adjusted" person. In other words, those who meet the expectations laid upon them by outside influences are "healthy." Those who fail to meet society's expectations in various ways are given any of a number of diagnoses, all suggesting disease, which is failure of adaptation.

The key here is that the "healthy" person—whether one is speaking of physical or mental/emotional health—is, according to this prevailing model, simply a person without disease. There is no concept of health in the broader sense beyond the adaptive one. In contrast, the model that informs this book, and the elements in it, is based not on the eradication of neurosis but on the embracing of the nearly unlimited potential for creativity, vitality, love, and passion.

The Big Three of our Inner World: Soul, Divinity, Ego

To further understand the differences between these models, it is important to recognize that the prevailing model is based on the profoundly limited assumption that we are simply our ego—and that our psychological health is simply the health of our ego. In fact, our inner world of mind, emotion, and spirit can be said to consist of three parts, our soul, our sense of divinity, and our ego. Of these, our ego is the most superficial among them. Let's explore this inner triumvirate more deeply.

You and I were born with the potential to be magnificently creative and expressive beings. Embedded in each of us is a unique voice aching to be realized. It can be called our soul—and I will often refer to it by that name here—but I am not referring to it in quite the same way that our familiar religious traditions might speak of it. Instead, I am referring to the soul as simply the deepest part of who we are. Metaphorically, it is our heart of hearts, and when we live from this place, our capacity for joy and satisfaction is boundless. Our soul is our unique expression of ourselves—a voice unlike any other. It is far more than the coding of our DNA that results in our becoming a particular form. It's as if we each see life through a unique lens, have a unique set of desires, and express ourselves in a unique way. Our voices and inflections are different; our physical rhythms, tempos, and energies are uniquely our own. Our beliefs and viewpoints occur in that exact combination only in ourselves. And our way of seeing and experiencing the world is different. The totality of these elements are driven by and expressions of our deepest soul.

An Exercise

Take a moment and reflect on your life. As you were growing up, what did you do particularly well? (You may or may not have noticed or been told of these things then.) Jot down these thoughts in your journal.

Now consider what you enjoyed doing the most. Think about times in which you felt most like you were in your element, expressing who you were or were meant to be. What were you doing then that made those times so special? Describe those times and activities in your journal.

While not conclusive, your responses to this exercise may begin to suggest your unique soul's expression. Note that it is not always what we do well that is our soul. Math came easy to me as a youth and I was quite good at it. It was never my soul's yearning. Sometimes our soul is best expressed as something that puts us in a state of enjoyment, openness, or appreciation of life, even if we haven't become skilled at it. On the other hand, we may be very skilled at certain things that do not reflect our soul's expression or our higher purpose. Sometimes it is simply a skill or aptitude that has us stand out. At this point you may already be noticing some clues about your soul's deepest desires for your own life. If so, jot them down in your journal.

Having a soul, with its unique purpose and yearning, only describes a part of what we are. We also were born with a natural sense of connection to all and everything. Some call it "being one with the universe." Carl Jung and his followers often refer to it as our collective consciousness, or Self with a capital "S". I think of it simply as our connection to the divine. By "divine," I am not necessarily referring to a traditional God concept. I mean divine in a broader (but still profound) sense—that we are a part of a larger system of energy that connects us together. Some who experience this might say that we are all "children of god." Whatever else it may mean, that metaphor refers to a connection to the universe in which one feels complete love, as if being held in its bountiful womb. In this sense, all of us are imbued with a divine quality, an essential goodness, and sense of fairness, justice, and love for all beings

The Next Exercise

Although we've all had moments in which this natural sense of peace, love, and connectedness—our divine connection—have been felt, we are not all equally aware of these moments. For some of us, such moments may be so far from our conscious thought patterns and identity that we cannot easily remember them. As a preparation for the following exercise (or simultaneously with the exercise), and as a goad to remembering, some of you might find it helpful to first get yourself in a receptive state, perhaps with relaxing music, a walk, or a quiet time of meditation or contemplation—whatever works.

The exercise itself is simple. Think about times when you felt most at peace and in love with the world. Note in your journal each event or moment and then write down what it felt like in that moment. Then reflect on these moments as to their meaning and their relevance for you in your life.

If you are like most people, what you're accessing are some combination of your deepest expression and your deepest connection. These two elements—our soul and our divinity (or divine connection)—are part of the natural way of things and they exist in all of us, whether we are able to see it or not. Moreover, they occupy center stage in our inner cosmology whether we are aware of them or not. Together, they form a powerful inner compass, a guiding light that too often we fail to honor and follow. When we embody these elements, we are experience natural inner freedom.

Amidst this powerful duo, we were also born with the seeds of an ego—the third part of our inner triumvirate. Once we understand how the ego grows and begins to take center stage in our inner cosmology while pushing aside our soul and our sense of divinity, we can then comprehend how we so often move from a state of natural joy early in life to one of neurosis, depression, and sometimes despair.

From the time of our birth, in addition to experiencing soul and connection, we also had two overriding instinctual needs—to be comfortable and to be loved. We popped out of the womb with no capability to provide for ourselves and so we relied solely on our parents (or primary caregivers) to provide for us.

If we were lucky, our parents did a decent job of raising us for the first few years. And if we were doubly lucky, their protective, loving shield was unconditional. Early on, we were amply held, coddled, and protected. Our parents nurtured us completely, and we felt safe within their sphere of protection. If our parents fully understood and embraced their function (in all its sacred and practical dimensions) in our early months, they choose to have us sleep in their bed, or at the very least right beside their beds, so we were not prematurely thrust into experiencing our separateness and vulnerability. Many native cultures understand this need well, as babies remain with their mothers at all times until ready to crawl and later walk. Crawling and walking are life's indicators that the child is ready for take small steps toward developing his or her unique and separate self.

Many of us were not so lucky. Perhaps our parents did not provide that love and security—either because of lack of understanding and connection, or because of their own lack of maturity. They set us up in our own room too soon out of some personally felt need to get away from the demands the child represents, or out of some misguided belief that it is in some way beneficial to force such independence on them before they are truly ready for it. At this early stage, children need the physical closeness to their parents; cribs with bars provide physical security but without the required closeness. When parents feel the need to get away from their children at these critical times in their development, it is our children who pay the price.

If we are particularly unfortunate, our parents or caretakers did not offer much tenderness either; in that case we have spent much of our life scarred or wounded from not getting what was most essential.

During our early years, our soul was quite actively communicating to us, and we often gave it heed. Our "soul needs" as young children expressed themselves as spontaneous exploration of the outer world and of ourselves—both of which were new to us. We needed adventure and we needed unedited expression.

Crawling is the beginning of this adventure—exploring our ability to move more freely, separate from others, and slowly developing our ability to take care of our own needs. Our physical mobility corresponded with a growing capacity to take care of our needs and to do what we (our separate self) wanted.

Somewhere around age one, give or take, we started to be shown and told that there were rules for living. Some of these rules, of course, were necessary for our safety. We could now walk and therefore might run into things and put ourselves at risk. We could move wherever we wanted to, so for our own protection (real or imagined by our parents), they told us "no" to any of a number of things. "No, you can't go there." "No, you can't touch that." "No you must not do that." Interestingly, the word "no" is one of the most common early words that come out of children's mouths, because it is what they hear the most.

An Exercise

Think back on the rules and restrictions you felt as a child. Pay particular attention to the rules that seemed to bind you—where some part of you was aching to express yourself or be free but the adults in your life said "no." What were some of those? Please write them down in your journal. List as many as come to mind easily. (Consider not only the rules that were explicitly stated, but also those that were implied and perhaps enforced through more subtle ways.)

The rules your listed in your journal were the first impressions of the culture beginning to shape you. Soon there were many more types of "no's" and they involved much more than our physical protection. These came in the form of "shoulds" or "shouldn'ts". As soon as we were able to comprehend it, we started to hear rules about what good little boys and girls are supposed to do. "Be a good girl, and mind your manners." "Good boys don't do that." Since we still needed the love and security that had once been given to us unconditionally, we did what we could to re-achieve that state—and that meant being good in the eyes of our parents and receiving their love and approval. When we didn't follow these rules, we were certain to get a consequence. Somewhere around this time, the ego began to take root—and it had to, in part, in order to claim a secure and rewarding place in life's unfolding drama.

Around age two, we began to individuate—to feel our own sense of ourselves as a unique being, separate from our parents. In the child's development, the individuated self starts with the ability to say "no" to our parents and follow our own desires. I believe that when kids during their supposed "terrible twos" throw temper tantrums, it is because their own self-expression is aching to get out. These tantrums often express our soul's need to be heard, witnessed, and honored. Too often parents squelch these desires for self-expression. Out of their own inability to be okay with the screams or deal with us in a tender manner, they tried to force us into "acceptable" behavior, either through punishment or through the withholding of overt expressions of love. Similarly, they offered rewards or loving actions when we did behave.

Since the primary purpose of the ego is to protect ourselves from harm from the outside world, our ego figured out that in order to be safe from our parents' or caregivers' punishment and in order to feel that succulent experience of love, we'd better follow the rules.

I remember a time when my son was around two-and-a-half years old that was wonderfully illustrative of the tension between his ego's needs to control his choices and the expectations I as a parent had. He was looking through a picture book in the car as we were driving some-where. Just as we arrived, I said to him, "Okay, Josh, let's go."

"No," he replied, "I want to finish."

"We don't have time, Josh, we've got to go," I retorted, a bit impatiently.

"I'm not done," he responded with equal strength.

I insisted once again and threatened to take the book away if he did not put it down on his own. So he rifled through the rest of the pages in a couple of seconds and then proudly declared, "Okay, Daddy, I'm done now."

As we were designed to do, he took the path of least resistance, which is to avoid pain or to seek pleasure. In this case he did both. He met my need but at the same time maintained some semblance of dig-nity and met his own need to finish in the only way he could figure out. His ego cleverly maintained his right to be right. And he did it in such a way that he would avoid my growing anger and hold on to my approval.

The greatest pain or pleasure in a young child's body is the loss or gain of the attention and love of our parents or primary caregivers. Later, in order to protect ourselves, our ego also adopted other strate-gies. But the primary one for now was to do what we were told and thereby get our parents' approval.

Most parents attempt to bend their young children to their will as I tried to do with my son in the car. Since our parents were also once chil-dren whose own parents most likely did a less-than-exemplary job of parenting, their childhood traumas become a part of their adult selves—so parents are like much bigger, more powerful, more strong-willed children. Too often, in their own insecurity, parents try to mold their children into their own perceived image, or into who they wished they had become, or who they wanted others to see them as. "I didn't get the education I wanted, so by God, I'm going to be sure you get yours, so study hard." "Become a doctor and then you'll do me proud." "You'll do as you're told, young lady. Do you want to embarrass me in front of our neighbors?" As a result of this nearly constant external pressure, most of our energy went into ego-survival issues, and our soul's desire became buried deep in the recesses of our unconscious mind.

When we went off to day care or to school for the first time, we learned of another power far greater than our own—the power of the community. This "community" involved two very powerful groups: teachers (or authority figures) and peers. The pressure from both of these groups was enormous, if often contradictory (peer pressure often moving in the opposite direction from authority pressure). Peter Berger, a brilliant sociologist with whom I had the honor to be a teaching assistant in graduate school, referred to the inescapable power of culture and community to mold us. I still vividly remember him pounding his fist on the table for emphasis as he declared in a strong German accent that matched his gestures, "Social norms and expectations are extraordinarily powerful [SLAM!]. The culture has a social facticity [SLAM!] not to be denied [SLAM!]."

An Exercise

Think of different spheres of influence in your childhood—school, family, friends, the media, church or religious institution, and broader community—and how each part put pressure on you, whether you knew it at the time or not. Consider what messages you received from these people concerning how to live and what to think. For each, jot down in your journal your sense of what they told you. Pay particular attention to the messages that felt constraining or limiting. Note the "shoulds" that you did not resonate with. For this exercise, it might be particularly useful to identify each sphere of influence and write down the unique messages from that sphere.

While it cannot be denied, "social facticity" can be overcome, but it requires a comprehension of our situation as powerful if not more powerful than the societal expectations to which we adapted ourselves. Of course, this is not easy, as our teachers, whatever their effectiveness as teachers, were often very effective at defining proper behavior. Our growing ego, quite active by this time, figured out that to get along and to get rewarded for being a good boy or girl, we needed to follow the rules. And in a certain limited sense that response was wise. Although our ego did an all-too-good job of hiding our tender soul and sense of divinity even from ourselves, it also served a protective function by giving us certain survival skills in the world. But as we mature we may at last begin to see the limits of its value and put the ego in its place. We can loosen the shackles of identification with this superficial survival mechanism, and thereby discover—buried beneath the ego—our true shape, destiny, and divine purpose.

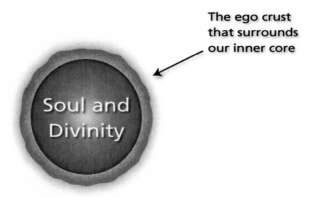

The ego crust that surrounds our inner core

Soul and Divinity

The problem of adult authorities pulling in one direction and peers (augmented by mass media) in a somewhat different direction left little room for us to follow our own inner guidance system. Any child that strayed from the group and tried to express himself was told in no uncertain terms what a problem he or she was. And so we followed, in lockstep with these external messages. This was our ego's best coping strategy. Unwilling and unable to deal with not being accepted, we tried to fit in.

Much of our schooling was not about finding our own unique voice but about memorizing the voice of others. Interestingly, the word "education" comes from the Latin word "educare," which literally means to draw out of. Unfortunately, the education we receive often has more to do with making "good citizens" out of us, or adding certain skill sets to the workforce, than with drawing out our extraordinary and unique gifts.

And so the pressure to conform continued throughout grade school and into high school and even college. As we continued to grow, we wrote papers, took tests, followed rules—all designed to make us good students and good citizens and meet our ego's needs to get ahead. For the few that make it there, it is only in graduate school that independent thinking is invited. But even then, there are strict protocols requiring that we build on the research of others, so that original thought that is not derivative is not seen as academically respectable. (This is true not only in graduate school but throughout the area of academic scholarship.) My doctoral dissertation, like most others, was riddled with references to others' research, and I felt proud in my ability to "know" my subject matter. What I knew was other people's views and research while struggling mightily to find my own.

As a side note: It is extraordinarily ironic to me that the teachers of our system of higher education who received doctorates are the ones who reached the pinnacle as students where adding something unique to prior research was an important test of their skill. They pass and then are qualified to mold others. Too often some of the finest thinkers stand in front of podiums and lecture to students, failing to remember that success was in finding one's own expression as opposed to telling others what is true or not true, what is right or what is wrong.

Defending Against an Illusion

Whenever ambition, need, expectation and personal desire are activated, we are under the ego's domination, and soul and divinity are taking a back seat. We carry around a minefield of wounds from long ago that get unconsciously triggered and re-stimulated, often as anger or defensiveness. We may or may not be aware of this in any given instance; but in every moment in which we regress to an immature state and act petulant, resentful, or deeply hurt, we can be assured that our ego has activated these responses.

The ego, in doing its job, expresses anger and defensiveness as a protection against felt pain, loss, or unmet need. The anger feels real and appropriate, yet our feelings are not really a direct response to our current experience, but were triggered by an old wound from a time long past. Whenever you feel anger, ask yourself, what might be the pain underneath that anger? Often you will find a tender wound or an unmet need, which is a form of a pain or hurt. In defense of that pain or loss or unmet need, our ego forms coping mechanisms in the form of anger or withdrawal. Our ego is our armor steeling oneself against the perceived source of the attack or threat. And the threat is, more often than not, an illusion.

I was sitting with a client one day in his office, which had a huge window that was mirrored on the outside, so that we could see out, but others could not see in. As we were conversing, a bird crashed into the window and died. The suddenness and violence of it all came as a shock to me. My client commented that this was quite a frequent event. He explained that as a bird flies toward its own image in the mirror, it perceives that it is being attacked by another bird, and in turn defends itself by attacking its own reflection. It occurred to me that this is remarkably similar to how we attack others when we experience them attacking us. More often than not, they are just coping with their own life, acting without necessarily being aware of the impact on us. And yet we take it personally, and so we "defend" ourselves by attacking back. What if their attack is just an illusion? What if the "attacker" is just a reflection of our self?

Not only do we allow perceived events to act as a sudden trigger that activates old wounds and brings the ego's arsenal of defense strategies to a state of attention, in like manner our ambitions also trigger our ego. In a world where success is defined in terms of what you own, how you are perceived, and the power you have over others, the ego's job becomes to get what it believes we need, based on society's definitions of need. We seek out success—or what society defines as success—as a way to feel seen, valued and even loved. To the extent that we don't already feel seen, valued and loved for who we are and not for what we do, our egos reign supreme.

An Exercise

Think back on your childhood and early adulthood and the myriad of ways in which you acted out or defended against difficult circumstances. List them in your journal and do your best not to judge them as problematic or wrong. Acting out can also be a cry to be witnessed, seen, or honored. It can be some part of you aching to be heard. Defenses are ways the ego behaves in order to protect something important to our sense of separate self.

These ego-driven strategies make up the drama of our lives, and yet they are fundamentally false responses based on dangers that do not exist—like the bird that fears its own reflection in a window and ends up inadvertently killing itself by not perceiving the true danger: the window itself. Not only are we reacting to false dangers, but the "self" we are protecting—the ego—is false as well. It is not all of who we are, and to believe it is takes us on a path that fails to access the deeper wellspring of existence that is both our birthright and the source of greater and more enduring fulfillment in life. By identifying exclusively with the ego structure, we miss out on these deeper treasures, which are like a transparent pool hidden beneath the crust that is the ego. In Western society, we live in a world made up by our egos, for our egos. At best, our ego can drive us to success (as defined by society), but it cannot drive us to fulfillment. Only our soul can.

But who speaks for the soul? Our ego certainly cannot, for its attention is on other things. Our culture cannot, for it is, to a large extent, a reflection of our collective ego desires for material success. And others typically cannot, for—as in our own case—their own souls are often crying to be heard by them.

You must speak for your own soul. To become fulfilled means to seek to rediscover that aspect of yourself that in all likelihood has lain dormant and claim it as your own. It is, according to Jung and many other observers of the human condition, necessary to one's own unfolding that one become individuated—in other words, to fulfill the soul's desire and express oneself as a unique human being—a "spark of divinity."

To the extent that you are able to have your soul's desire be your guiding light, you will lead a grounded, easy, satisfying and joyous life, steeped in divine purpose.

An Exercise

Take a moment and reflect on your life. Do you know what your calling is? Do you know your heart's deepest desire? Write in your journal some possibilities, without attachment to any one of them.

Now reflect on this list. Are your desires truly your own—or have you bought into the messages society has given us about what the good life is? Are your deepest convictions and beliefs the fruit of personal experience and consideration, or are they inherited or taken on from others? Have you examined the ways you relate to external authority and found your own truth? Write down your thoughts to these questions in your journal.

On the basis of these questions and this chapter, are you clear about what stands between the life you are leading now and the full and passionate life you were meant to live? Write your thoughts in your journal and treat them as emerging rather than cast in stone. New insights may come through you as you read further and as a result of subsequent exercises. Please be sure to update your images, thoughts, and impressions of blockages as you go.

Reflect on this list. Are your desires truly your own—or have you bought into the messages society has given us about what the good life is? Are your deepest convictions and beliefs the fruit of personal experience and consideration, or are they inherited or taken on from others? Have you examined the ways you relate to external authority and found your own truth? Write down your thoughts to these questions here below.

On the basis of these questions and this chapter, are you clear about what stands between the life you are leading now and the full and passionate life you were meant to live? Write your thoughts here.

CHAPTER TWO

THE EXPERIENCE OF AUTHENTICITY

"If a man does not keep pace with his companions,
perhaps it is because he hears a different drummer.
Let him step to the music which he hears,
however measured or far away."

– Henry David Thoreau

At the deepest level of who we are there lies stillness, an inner peace, a knowing that all that we are is connected to everything else. When we are at peace with ourselves in this way, without a need to become something, we begin to connect with our soul's deepest yearnings. When we live from within and express these desires, we feel alive and full, and at one with (rather than threatened by) others and their success.

We have all experienced this feeling at one time or another, however fleeting it may have been. As a child we knew this state well. We experienced it as a place of freedom, aliveness, joy—as a place where magic was simply a given, because there were no limits to the possible.

As adults most of us seem no longer able to contact that state at will. Some of us can't seem to find it at all, or we don't even think to look for it—but it's still there. We may come across it accidentally. It may appear unbidden during periods of intense creativity, when all effort seems to cease and we find ourselves "in the flow"—extraordinarily productive, creative, and expressive.

This sense of total peace and total connection may also appear at a moment of intimacy with a loved one, when suddenly there is no separation and no time, and the other's eyes become a window to the joy and light that are at the heart of oneself. And it also appears when a person expresses herself fully, unencumbered by thoughts about what people will think. Witness the extraordinary beauty of someone bursting out in song in a crowd and feeling and expressing life's glory. Consider the breathless joy of a child who bursts out in laughter at the simplest of things—or the transformative experience of someone who speaks about their pain vulnerably while all else around are posturing and protecting.

This ultimate but elusive state of grace is recognized in the highest mystical traditions of every major religion, East and West, from aboriginal communities to monasteries and ashrams. It is also recognized in many modern traditions and in transpersonal psychology. Although most of us are strangers to our core self and our soul's calling (at least most of the time), the experience of the core self is universal—that is, it crosses all boundaries of religion, culture, and worldview—and it is universally valued among those who have experienced it. While the soul's calling may be different in each of us, we all share the phenomenon of its presence.

Over the years, through a series of conscious and unconscious choices in which ego took over, we moved away from that place and learned how to conform to the expectations of society. In other words, we learned what it means to be "normal." In this process of conditioning, our ego asserted its prominence and took us further away from our deeper, more natural state of being. While perhaps more productive, we also lost our ability to access those primary energies that were once so familiar to us. We forgot who we are and what makes our heart sing.

There is a song I recently heard, written by George Strait, whose title is: "I Thought I Heard You Calling My Name." It is a simple and powerful song about a person who lost a lover, and keeps sensing the lover might come back. Repeated over and over is the phrase: "I heard you call my name." Taken literally, the song is about a real lover whose presence is sensed or hoped; but, taken in a different way, it could be about a person sensing that the long-lost soul of the lover is finally calling out to him or her. It is the whisper of the yearning of the soul for you to come home, to come back to the soul.

Those who are truly fulfilled are able to comfortably and quickly find and act from their own inner home, they are good with themselves and with who they are, and they interact with others in a way that helps others find the same self-acceptance and satisfaction. This capacity to act from one's core and inspire others to do the same is more than a skill, a theory, or a model. Grounded in a deep sense of self, it's a way of being.

Authenticity is the experience of living life in the raw, with eyes and heart wide-open, fully embracing life's innate joy and fully experiencing heartbreak, caring more for our deeper soul's expression than for our momentary and fleeting preferences and the demands of our ego's desires. Make no mistake about it, though. Living authentically is by definition quite vulnerable. By tapping into our deepest truths about ourselves, we are exposing ourselves to the potential ridicule of others as well as to uncomfortable but often valuable feedback. It means receiving unflattering revelations about ourselves, and also discovering the hollowness of a culture that may have once provided meaning and comfort.

Concern with what others will think can greatly inhibit our growth. To say to someone, "I deeply desire to be a musician," especially when there is little evidence that we have talent, exposes us to risk silent or even overt ridicule. Most crucially, we expose ourselves to another person's belief about whether fulfilling our heart's desire is practical or even possible. If that person does not believe we can, she will say so with her body or her words. Her words might say "That's nice," but by the absence of active encouragement or enthusiasm in her voice, we sense we are being told in effect that it is not a worthy or wise aspiration.

Similarly, to say to a date "I like you and want to see you again" runs the risk he or she will say no directly or indirectly. And so our desire is exposed. To express our most raw feelings of anger or hurt or deep sadness and despair runs the risk that others will not hold us with kindness and warmth, and so we are left feeling alone.

And yet, to live authentically means that we acknowledge and express the desires, yearnings, and sheer joy of our deepest self—to ourselves and to others, moment by moment—knowing others may reject or avoid us. From the ego's vantage point, living authentically seems very risky; but if we're not willing to take that perceived risk, the truth of who we are, what we want, and how we feel goes underground, protected by layers of armor, to the point that we no longer have easy access to it. The true risk, then, is that by ignoring the soul's needs, the soul's life and expression get smothered under a lifetime of armoring, and as a result we are no longer in communication with our deepest self.

To live fully requires we step out of the inner boundaries and let go of life as we've known it. To live fully means we have to face ridicule and rejection. I am reminded of a poem by Rumi, the great Sufi Poet, who wrote:

> For years, copying other people,
> I tried to know myself.
> From within, I couldn't decide what to do.
> Unable to see, I heard my name being called.
> Then I walked outside.
> The breeze at dawn has secrets to tell you;
> Don't go back to sleep.
> You must ask for what you really want;
> Don't go back to sleep.
> People are going back and forth across
> the doorsill where the two world touch.
> The door is round and open.
> Don't go back to sleep.

For years, copying other people, I tried to know myself. From within, I couldn't decide what to do.

To live life authentically requires that we at least recognize that the source of our despair or lack of fulfillment may go far deeper than mere frustration of the ego's desire or cravings; in fact, it may be rooted in a lost connection with our soul. Our soul seems to live outside the doorway of awareness and we go asleep to its existence. This loss of soul connection is nearly universal, and it almost always occurs unconsciously in response to outside pressures placed on the ego. As we proceed to uncover and heal this separation, it is important that we simply observe and understand the choices we made, without judgment or condemnation. Sad or unpleasant feelings may arise, but whatever we feel is okay. We should allow the feelings to deepen, and explore their rich contours, all the while remaining in a place of compassion with ourselves and with others. Only when we have done this are we able to live life fully, with passion and open-heartedness. Then and only then can we experience true and enduring intimacy with ourselves and with another.

An Exercise

Think back on a time in your life when you wanted something, or wanted to do something, and for whatever reason, you decided you wouldn't or couldn't. Write it down in your journal.

Now think about what stopped you—typically a thought, fear, or belief—and write it down in your journal, preferably right next to the prior entry.

Now consider what you wrote. Ask yourself, to what extent was it buying into a belief that your community, family, or friends had? In this process, you are making an unconscious choice to trust something other than your deeper self. You faced what we all face, hundreds of times—a conflict between trusting your soul and trusting the group around you. And in many ways, it was your ego protecting you from facing the potential of being ostracized from the group. In deciding against your own deeper desires and feelings, what beliefs did you acquire from others and integrate into yourself? Write those beliefs in your journal now.

People who live a fully authentic life implicitly trust their inner guidance, and hence are not at conflict with themselves. They are living the spirit called forth in William Ernest Henley's poem Invictus which concludes "I am the master of my fate: I am the captain of my soul."

The deep quality that distinguishes people who are truly fulfilled from the rest of us is the power of connecting with and heeding the directions of one's own internal guidance system. The experience of authenticity is extraordinarily freeing. In contrast to second-guessing themselves and others, worrying about how they will be received, feeling as if they are walking on eggshells, or feeling self-conscious, they simply flow in life, maturely expressing their truth, and welcoming others to do the same. Such an experience allows for ease, comfort, and full accessibility to the range of experiences available in life without self-editing or being concerned with others' reactions.

This lack of self-editing often takes the form of rebellion in one's early years, and many such individuals can be described as nonconformists. In a fascinating study by George Valliant, written about in his classic book Adaptation to Life, he discovered that many if not most highly successful leaders bucked the trend when they were young. Many were misfits, not able to fit in well with their fellow students. They were often troublemakers, and many did not learn their "lessons" well. They may have learned what "normal" meant, but something inside of them chose not to be "normal."

It's as if they knew early on they needed to follow their unique voice. Great leaders are pathfinders, not path followers, and to find a new and perhaps greater path, one needs to be willing to stray. To the leader, it does not feel like straying at all. It feels more like following one's own inner guidance system.

It is interesting that so many successful leaders found it necessary in their formative years to buck a system whose very purpose is to create society's leaders! How many more great leaders might we have if we had an educational system that actually encouraged independent thinking and new ideas? It is not only leaders that have powerful inner guidance systems—we all do. But, for many of us the outer "system" that was foisted on us did an outstanding job of burying our spontaneity, creativity, and deeper desires.

Nonconformity and a rebellious nature make up just one side of the authentic life. People who live authentically also accept the natural vulnerability that is associated with it. There is an underlying self-esteem that can bear the weight of this exposure. Because they feel at peace with themselves, when others reject them for what they see, feel or believe, the hurt from that rejection or judgment is but a momentary experience. It is a reminder that we are all tender in some way and that we have past wounds that are not yet fully healed and may never be. The person who is committed to a path of authenticity will be curious about her own pain and may even go into the feeling to deepen her awareness. In so doing, the pain of the past is re-experienced for a moment, but then it disappears, as if by magic. Just like the feeling that emerges after a good cry—one of release and even happiness—the full experience of any feeling releases us from its bondage.

Mark Twain once quipped that he preferred to always tell the truth because it did not require he remember anything. Such is the spirit of the person living an authentic life. The truth is always welcome no matter what. I can experience what is true in this moment and express it, taking care to offer it to another person in a way that it can easily be received.

This last qualification—that it be easily received—is an important one. Because part of my truth is that I never impose it on another and I care about others' wellbeing, when my truth has something to do with another person, I don't simply blurt it out. I take care in its expression, for I care about its impact on others. Too often people confuse authenticity with expressing everything they feel, no matter what, and in the form they feel it. In the name of honesty, they become emotional bullies. They may feel better for having released a pent-up emotion, but they leave a bitter wake behind them. That is not authenticity; it is trampling on another's spirit.

The experience of authenticity is a dance of speaking our must vulnerable truths and being curious about self and other. It is a dance of owning all of who we are and seeking to find its full expression. An authentic relationship is one with no holds barred—it includes joy, anger, belly-pulsating laughter and heartbreaking despair, rapture and disgust—any expression that is consistent with our deepest feelings and integrity. Such a relationship becomes a dance of curiosity and revelation and joyous acceptance in the discovery of whatever is true. Such a relationship with oneself and with another is certainly the exception, but in many ways it is the sine qua non of an authentic life.

Up until about seven years ago I have been both gifted and afflicted with an ability to rein in many emotions and keep them quiet, especially feelings of frustration and anger. The beauty of it is that I am perceived and confided in as a kind person, and people feel safe with me. The curse, however, is that I have had difficulty accessing, feeling, expressing, and releasing strongly held emotions, and so they stay locked within. Along with this tendency, I have lived most of my life somewhat stiffly. Just as I didn't feel too much anger, the heights of joy had also, for much of my life, eluded me.

Picture it this way. Imagine we each have a range of emotions from +10 (extraordinary joy and happiness) to -10 (extraordinary sadness or violent anger). My pattern for most of my life has been to live somewhere in the +4 to −4 range. Every now and then I'd have an unusual moment of expression in either direction, but these moments fell outside of the bell-shaped curve of my typically felt and expressed life. To many, and to some extent to myself, I appeared buttoned-down and well contained. The problem was that, along with my strong capacity for emotional moderation came a concomitant inability to fully drink in the nectar that life offers.

An Exercise

What is the range in which you live your life? Seven years ago, I reflected on this question and this is how I depicted my life:

Keith's range of emotions

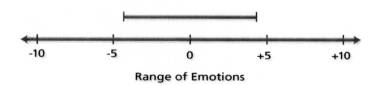

Range of Emotions

Now, write yours in your journal using the image below as a guide.

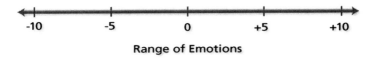

Range of Emotions

And if your behaviors and feelings were to be depicted such that you'd see the skew of your own feelings, what would the skew look like? Below is a depiction of mine seven years ago.

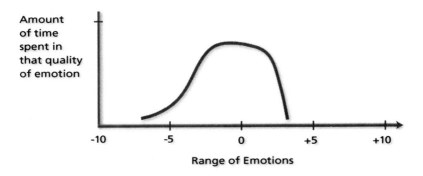

Range of Emotions

Each of us has our own unique pattern. Note that I was usually at peace, close to the neutral range. Neutral is not good or bad in this exploration. One could easily say I wasn't really neutral anyway; I was flat! My life-energy was dampened, preventing the direct experience of stronger emotions and maybe even vitality. Many of us have double or even triple humps on the skew. Your pattern should not be judged as "good" or "bad." Simply discovering what is true for you is itself the beginning of liberation from the limitations of your pattern. In your journal, draw your own skew. As you do, in this case, and in all other time, you are simply being invited to honor the truth, without self-judgment.

Now reflect on this question: What does this skew say about you? Write down your musings in your journal.

INNER FREEDOM

Consider that if you are tilted in one direction or another, you might be disowning or disconnected from its opposite. Most often people who believe they are happy, for example, are simply trying to put a positive face on their lives and end up feeling "plastic"—not really honoring what is so. It is folly to believe we can live a life where all we feel are the upsides of emotions and not the downsides. To live such a life requires that we tell ourselves certain emotions are not okay. When we do, the negative emotions go underground to simmer in the deep recesses of our hearts and minds, where they create a kind of acidity in our bodily experience and in our words and deeds.

Another symptom of buried emotions is a face that is hardened or frozen with worry or anguish. We may also appear physically or mentally rigid—oh-so-careful to avoid saying certain things. Our negative emotions may not be spoken or directly felt by us, but they emanate from our pores and wreak havoc on our bodies. I believe that many chronic medical problems are a result of many years of not experiencing or expressing—and therefore not being able to let go of—the emotions to which we have denied ourselves access because they are "not okay."

Similarly, it is folly to believe that the imprint of sadness that you and others feel constantly is your natural state of being—although it might feel that way after so long embodying the more negative state of emotions. People who constantly feel sour, angry, and frustrated are often disconnected from the more positive experience inside themselves. They have disowned joy, ease, and happiness.

Years ago, having noticed the pattern of constriction that had marked my adult life, I decided to experiment for a while by living life on the edge. I gave myself the task of expressing any and all emotions, no matter what they were, and no matter what the circumstance. The only boundary I put on it was in my work, where it might put me or others at significant risk were I to share my emotions fully. Even there, though, I choose to go well beyond the limits of what was "acceptable" to me in my past patterning. With my friends and family and casual acquaintances, I put no such boundaries on myself. Even if I had an emotion relative to a total stranger, I would express it.

I did this experiment for a week and noticed an immediate and powerful quickening of my step and felt much more at ease in my body. I also became immediately aware of the fears that were present after my emotions were expressed. I felt enormously vulnerable and equally alive. I decided to continue the experiment for another week, and then another, and then another, to the point that a palpable and enduring shift had occurred. Now I live comfortably in roughly a +7 to −7 range. I say this with a smile on my face knowing the range is not at all precise, but it is enjoyable imagining it being so. Amusement aside, the range is much wider than before, and my feelings of joy and tenderness have increased proportionately. While I may never reach the full range of experience, I am happily committed to an ever more expansive and deepening process.

Finding Our Inner Authority

To live authentically is very simple in principle, and yet extraordinarily hard to do. It means following your own heart and finding your unique view of life. It means being opened up to a new way of seeing the world and life—a way that no one taught you, but that you must discover through your own experience and through the soul's recognition. It means choosing a path that is your own based on your own insight into yourself, rather than on someone else's idea of what you should be. It requires paying attention to your own inner authority, rather than blindly accepting the cultural "downloads" of outer authorities, such as parents (or the still-active "parental" voice instilled by your upbringing), peers, teachers, mass media, and popular culture.

Interestingly, the term "authority" has embedded in it the root word "author." To be the author of our own lives means that we're our own inventor. Inventors create, and to create means to do something no one else has done. To be the author of our own lives means to express our selves uniquely and unequivocally. When we see others who appear to be true authorities, it is often not because they hold a particular position, although they often do. It is because they come across as having gravitas—a weight about them. This comes from their own inner authority, not by the power that the position bestows on them. This is our birthright: to be the author of our lives, to live our life guided by our own inner compass.

Once we come to a recognition that our soul has been trampled by the dictates of our ego, and that these dictates came not from within but from forces outside of us, we then owe it to ourselves to recover our soul and our divine purpose. If indeed we made an unconscious choice to internalize these dictates, then recognizing we were the ones who lost sight of our own soul gives us power and freedom to choose differently now, at this moment of awareness.

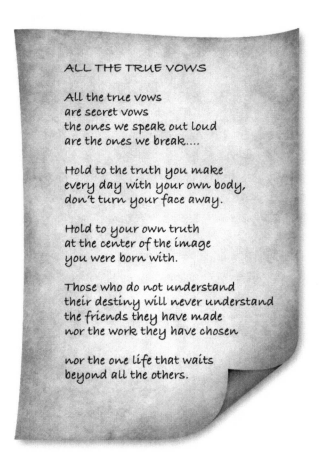

ALL THE TRUE VOWS

All the true vows
are secret vows
the ones we speak out loud
are the ones we break....

Hold to the truth you make
every day with your own body,
don't turn your face away.

Hold to your own truth
at the center of the image
you were born with.

Those who do not understand
their destiny will never understand
the friends they have made
nor the work they have chosen

nor the one life that waits
beyond all the others.

To do this is effectively to make a vow—a vow to your own deepest self. This vow is not like a contract based on external obligation. Rather, it is based on deep, recognized necessity. It may go something like this (but it is most important that the words resonate with you): "I vow to follow my own inner muse, at all moments and in every way. I vow not to stray from my true and deepest calling. I vow to honor my views and give them expression. And because I know that being fulfilled in life requires this, I also vow to honor others as they express who they are." This is the most important vow we can make, because it is a vow generated from within ourselves, as the accompanying poem by David Whyte reminds us. By keeping this vow, we will find riches aplenty on this earth, and we will live a truly satisfying life.

An Exercise

I encourage you to experiment for yourself for a week in a manner similar to my own experiment in which I purposely expressed all my emotions to everyone, as described above. You can do it in either of two ways. The first way is the boldest and potentially the scariest. Go for a week expressing all and everything. Of course, where there is potential for damage or for others to go into deep reaction, take good care that it is expressed in a way that it can be heard and accepted. With some people in your

CHAPTER THREE

THE SYMPTOMS OF INAUTHENTICITY

"I have spent my days stringing and unstringing my instrument while the song I came to sing remains unsung."

— Rabindranath Tagore

In a Washington, D.C. Metro station on a cold January morning in 2007, a man with a violin played six Bach pieces. Unbeknownst to the walkers-by, that man was the world-renowned violinist Joshua Bell, playing incognito.

Few stopped to listen—27 to be exact. Even fewer offered him money in spite of the fact that he played for 43 minutes some of the most astounding and difficult violin pieces known to mankind. He earned $57 for his performance that day. Two days before, Bell sold out a theater in Boston where the seats averaged $100.

Too often we miss the beauty that surrounds us day to day. We fall prey to the humdrum buzz of life and fail to see its remarkable contours. We have become numb to our extraordinary existence.

There are signs all around us of inauthenticity, and we pay a heavy price for participating in it. People who live their lives from a place of deep integrity and authenticity can see the signs easily. Most of us don't. The most frequent signs are ennui or depression, self-destructive habits (including the need to numb oneself), and violent anger.

Depression and Ennui

In our Western society, we live in a culture of depression. Here are a few unsettling facts:

- Published studies report that about 25% of all U.S. adults have a mental illness and that nearly 50% of U.S. adults will develop at least one mental illness during their lifetime.[2]

- 25% of those who suffer a mental disorder suffer from a serious mental illness. In addition, mental disorders are the leading cause of disability in the U.S. and Canada for ages 15-44.[3]

- Perhaps even more disturbing is the prevalence of mental health problems among our youth. In 2011, more than one in four (29 percent) high school students in grades 9-12 who participated in a national school-based survey reported feeling sad or hopeless almost every day for two weeks or longer during the past year—a red flag for possible clinical depression.[4]

- Mental illnesses account for more disability in developed countries than any other group of illnesses, including cancer and heart disease.[5]

- In 2006, 33,300 (approximately 11 per 100,000) people died by suicide in the U.S. By the year 2010, that number increased to 38, 364 (12.4 per 100,000).[6]

- More than 90 percent of people who kill themselves have a diagnosable mental disorder, most commonly a depressive disorder or a substance abuse disorder.[7]

In the face of these conditions, not long ago many of us turned to a psychiatrist for guidance and psychotherapy. Today when we go to a psychiatrist, chances are it is for a pill to try to overcome the chemistry of depression. Annual sales of antidepressants have nearly tripled since 1997, and there is no end in sight. Driven by the prevalent diagnosis that depression is caused by chemical imbalance or by genetics, millions of people take what appears like the logical remedy for what ails them—a pill. Well over 10% of the adult U.S. population have chosen this remedy, and it appears to work, often spectacularly well. One can feel the rapid lift of emotions as the pill hits our brain and ramps up our serotonin levels. The resulting changes in the brain's chemistry seem to confirm that the chemistry caused the depression in the first place. And in a society that seeks rapid cures for chronic ailments, why not do what seems both effective and effortless: why not take a pill?

About ten years ago, I finally came to accept the fact that for years I had experienced mild depression. Never had the depression been strong enough to cause me much concern. It was an almost imperceptible light cloud that followed me wherever I went. At the time I suspected it might have been genetic, for almost all members of my family on both sides have had the same kind of affliction, some far worse than mine. And in a world where Prozac, Wellbutrin, Effexor and other drugs were rapidly considered acceptable, I decided to try the pharmaceutical solution myself.

I met with a psychiatrist who, after spending two-sessions with me, affirmed my self-diagnosis, and prescribed Wellbutrin. After hemming and hawing about my decision for a few days, I took the plunge. At first I felt nausea just as the psychiatrist had predicted, so I played with the dosage for a few weeks until I got it just right. It's amazing how our bodies are able to adjust to what is clearly a foreign and unwelcome toxic agent.

Oh how wonderful it felt! My spirits soared as I experienced, through the magic of brain science, a continually depression-free state for the first time in 25 years. The difference was indeed remarkable. I had a smile on my face week after week. Nothing seemed to get me down, and nothing seemed to bother me. I became a delight to be with, filled with humor and good cheer. And I enjoyed the feeling—in fact, I loved the feeling. It didn't even bother me that my libido was negatively affected (an often-experienced side effect), for the drug was a powerful tonic.

I might have continued to enjoy the effects of the medication indefinitely had an important event not hit me like a ton of bricks. Around this time, two of my best friends, a couple with whom my wife and I were extremely close, gave birth to a child that was afflicted with an enormous number of medical conditions. The combination rendered their newborn unable to ever walk, unlikely to ever grow beyond a two-year-old intelligence, and with a heart condition that would probably prove fatal within a few years. They were naturally devastated by this and shared their vulnerability with me.

Normally I would have been extraordinarily saddened and deeply empathetic about their current and future challenges, for I loved them dearly. But under the influence of Wellbutrin, none of this touched me at all. Of course, I said all the right words, but I couldn't feel anything other than the pleasure of my own life. That same evening, while having dinner with them shortly after hearing the news, I was laughing and joking as if nothing was the matter. Naturally, my friends observed this behavior and were more than perplexed with my seeming indifference and inappropriate lightheartedness. Being the good friends that they are, they provided me with honest feedback: "What's going on with you, Keith? It's as if you are not there." It's not that I was actually indifferent to their situation; it did matter, in my head, but my heart could not feel their pain.

The next day, it dawned on me what had happened, and I immediately threw out the drug. Being happy at the expense of being connected to my heart and to the people I love was not worth it. As a result, the all-too-familiar subtle signs of depression returned as quickly as they had been lifted; and for years more, I continued to feel this general malaise to which I was so accustomed.

Today, the depression is gone, and this happened without any additional drug regimens. This change didn't happen as a result of counseling or therapy, although those can help, nor was it due to an unexpected change in circumstances. A few years ago, I realized I was not living my life fully and authentically, and I needed to embrace fully who I was. It was then that I changed the focus of my consulting work. It was then that I separated from my wife, who I loved deeply but with whom I was caught in a powerful negative bonding pattern that we were both unable to break, despite years of continual effort. It was then that I finally relinquished the need to define myself as a good provider, measured by the size of our house and bank account. Until then, I felt the oppressive weight of pressure to keep earning high amounts of money so we could live comfortably in Marin County, California, whose cost of living is one of the highest in the United States. It was then that I began to write for my own pleasure and discover and express my unique gifts more fully. It was then that I let go of worldly ambition and sought to embrace my heart's deepest desires. And as I embraced who I was and how I wanted to be in the world, the cloud of depression lifted on its own. Three years later, it has not returned.

Depression, lethargy, and generalized anxiety are certainly complex forces with no single cause or solution. Whenever any of these conditions chronically and significantly affect one's life, one should be open to **all** possible causes, including a chemical imbalance. But consider the possibility that the chemical imbalance is caused by deeper patterns, one of which may be that your soul is aching for you to live the life of its own calling. My experience is that, almost without fail, people who create a major shift in their lives and choose to live their soul's purpose experience a far greater and enduring effect than you might have ever imagined to be possible—not just in their mood, but in the depths of their being where happiness truly resides.

Self-destructive Habits

There should be little if any doubt that there is a direct relationship between our society's habit of chasing short-term goals and immediate pleasures and the fact that we Americans are a nation of people who are among the most unhealthy of any "advanced" Western nations in body, mind, and soul. If you doubt that we are in a runaway health crisis, consider the huge recent increases in rates of obesity and crash dieting and eating disorders—or the vast increases in portion sizes and corresponding decrease in quality of foods consumed at a meal. Or consider the rise in diabetes, which I believe to be directly related to eating habits. With respect to obesity, in 2000, 27% of men and 33.4% of women were obese. 10 years later, those numbers increased to 35.5 and 35.8% respectively. These numbers have been severely increasing over the past few decades.[8] With respect to diabetes, The Centers for Disease Control and Prevention (CDC) analyzed data from two surveys conducted a decade apart—in 1995–1997 and 2005–2007—which showed a near-doubling of the incidence of diabetes in the later survey over the earlier one.[9] Similarly, the Gallup-Healthways Well-Being Index found shocking results in an 18-month study in 2008/09. This study showed that, by the third quarter of 2009, 11.3% of American adults—some 26 million Americans—had diabetes, up from 10.4% just 18 months earlier. If current trends continue, 15% of American adults will be living with diabetes by the end of 2015.[10] All of this points to the conclusion that we have a very unhealthy relationship with food, which is how we sustain our body—even as we become more and more obsessed with food and health!

Or consider the rates of violent crime and incarceration, which exceed by most measures every other country on Earth. Or consider the runaway consumer spending that savages the planet's future, teaches children that materialism is king, has contributed to the destruction of the economy, and has added nothing to our true happiness or well-being.

Perhaps most amazing of all, most of us are scarcely aware of how unwell we truly are, or of how we got that way. Deluged by ads of smiling people who tell us how they got rich quickly and how we can too, how they lost weight quickly and easily, and how they were taught to use escape clauses in the law to avoid paying debt, we stuff ourselves with these habits and beliefs (often justified as being part of the sacrosanct "American Dream") only to find that they never nurture our soul.

With our soul aching and the depression that ensues, the cycle of food binging and addictions of every kind only reinforces itself. Expert product marketing has even convinced us of the value of every new and expensive energy pick-me-up available on the market. In addition to the old standbys like coffee, lattes, and colas, there are now such drinks as Monster, The 5-Hour Energy Booster, Red Bull and the like. Without these jolts, we're left with the awareness that our life feels empty, without purpose and fulfillment.

The effects of consuming and depending on these foods and drugs are not unlike the effect of my antidepressant; I managed to escape my low-grade depression only to discover that I had lost my ability to feel. Unfortunately, for many this loss of ability to feel is so chronic and all consuming, and supported in so many ways by our friends and our culture, that it goes unnoticed altogether. Also supported and even encouraged by the culture is the use of these substances to keep us oblivious to our own pain. In addition to food, alcohol, caffeine, nicotine, and recreational drugs, we have become phenomenal users of prescription drugs, most of which have undesirable side effects especially when used in certain combinations. Adjusted for inflation, spending for prescription drugs increased roughly 10% per year from 1997 to 2007, and only recently has the rate of increase leveled off. Put another way, in ten years we doubled the number of drugs we were taking—resulting in a growth in prescription drug use that is three times that of healthcare spending in general.

Look at it this way. The country with the highest amount of wealth and technological advancement has an extraordinarily high amount of chronic disease and emotional dysfunction. Sadly, too few see the relationship between the two.

For a long time in my life, I could not see the relationship either. At age 22, I began to experience bleeding in my colon. Terrified, I went to my doctor, who referred me to the finest specialist in the country who treated such conditions. After a couple of tests, it was clear: I had ulcerative colitis, a condition that afflicts millions. It is a disease that has no known cause in Western medicine and no known cure. The bouts of bleeding can be frequent and terrifying, and if the pills to allay the symptoms don't work, the ultimate solution is removal of the colon. In addition to such suffering, those of us with more severe forms of the disease are more than 30 times as likely to get cancer of the colon as the average person. We all walk around with this awareness, and we think of it each time the bleeding and nausea come.

Whenever I had a such bleeding, I'd go to my doctor and he would prescribe a steroid solution. It is a severe response to a severe problem. Every time I'd ask: "Isn't there another way?" and he would say with great authority, "There is no known way of solving this." And so I believed him, taking ever-increasing dosages of pills (eventually up to 12 a day) to reduce the likelihood of symptoms arising, and then a steroid (a more attractive alternative than surgery) if the symptoms got dangerously severe. Naturally, over the years this medicine begins to affect the liver, but it is a devil's dilemma, and I chose the colon over the liver.

About ten years ago I made a commitment to myself to find a way to at least reduce the symptoms, if not affect a cure; so I began to investigate my own body to see if I could discover a clear pattern to the symptoms. It took a while, for I'd only have about one or two bouts a year, but each time the symptoms appeared I would pay very close attention to how the symptoms related to my body, outer events and circumstances, and my inner life. This, by the way, is how many ulcerative colitis sufferers address their symptoms. Unsatisfied with what Western medicine has given us, many of us have committed to discovering as much as we could on our own.

I started to notice that when I had bleeding, it was preceded by a fair degree of anxiety. Interestingly, up until fairly recently, I had not been fully in touch with my own anxiety. After a period of bleeding, though, if I looked back, I could see that I was anxious about something—a relationship with a client, the loss of some work (real or imagined), a failed effort of some kind. Throughout my life, being very driven to succeed, I often feared failure or, when making a mistake, became hard on myself. This would show up as anxiety, which caused me to remember the enormous anxiety I felt almost constantly as a child, the pressure of which drove me to high achievement. As I detected these patterns, I also started to remember that as a child I had had many stomachaches and wrenching episodes of food poisoning; and as an adult, I have been more susceptible to these problems than most people. In the past 25 years excruciating stomach pains have sent me to the hospital many times. I now attribute the childhood symptoms as well as the colitis to a heightened tendency toward anxiety. In researching this, I've since learned that in the Chinese system of medicine, there is a direct connection between anxiety and the stomach or intestinal region.

My experiences with colitis have taught me a great deal about the need to face myself and calm the inner storm. I have since also searched for other warning signals about my anxiety, and I've found two. I notice that when I'm anxious, I'm impatient, and so my impatient behavior is a clue to my inner world. This comes as no surprise. I've also noticed that when I'm anxious, my voice sounds constricted and higher—whereas when I'm fully relaxed, my voice is deep and resonant. The differences in my voice may often be too subtle for most people to take notice of. In fact, even though the connection between vocal characteristics and anxiety is well known, it is not something I had taken notice of until I began investigating bodily signs of my own anxiety. Because I'd often not been attentive to my own anxiety in the past, seeing these connections has provided me with a wonderful early warning signal, a barometer of my anxiety that is a daily teacher.

I have also since committed to a path of being more easy with myself, and through meditation and simple reminders, I find that I walk this Earth much more lightly. I include a daily morning practice as well as taking many moments throughout the day to simply deepen my breathing, connect to my body, and invite an open-hearted state of being. As a result of my efforts, I was able to reduce my colitis medication to a bare minimum, to which my gastroenterologist just shakes his head in wonder, treating my approach not as a clue to learning but as an unexplainable anomaly. Since then, I have done more research on my condition and found further dietary practices that have enabled me to no longer use the medicine at all. Where once I was told by my doctor I would probably have to take the maximum dosage for the rest of my life, and that it was better to live with a weak liver than to shorten my life by risking low medication, I now take no medication and have been symptom free for a year.

The habitual choices in our society to seek medical remedies that temporarily relieve symptoms and to stuff our mouths with foods that are clearly detrimental are self-destructive habits, pure and simple. They are habits born out of an inability to step back and notice the cycles of our addiction and denial. And beyond that, we have starved ourselves of the fulfillment (or even awareness) of our deepest purpose and most encompassing desires. Instead we heed only the most immediate desire to feel good, all the while not even noticing that we've "been there, done that". In fact, the reason we are not feeling good is (at least in large part) because these efforts that we're automatically repeating have failed every time. Put differently, we consistently trade long-term satisfaction for a short-term boost, and we are all too often unaware that we've made the trade.

Most tragically, this phenomenon applies not just to our individual lives but also to our entire society, which is living this paradigm on a mass scale. The most important decisions we make together as a community or as a country reveal the same pattern of addiction, denial, and myopia as the decisions we make for ourselves. And the tragedy that is befalling our society not only portends its own destruction if it continues unabated—it is also affecting us all now in countless ways, including (to cite one example among many) the seeming inability of our elected representatives as a group to act in our broader, long-term (or even broader immediate) interests. The problem with our short-term, feel-good solutions—whether they take the form of stuffing ourselves, having a drink, taking a drug (recreational or prescription), or (in the case of politicians) getting elected or re-elected—is that these fixes are all temporary salves against the deeper wound—that we are not living a natural and authentic life—and until we understand this pattern for what it is, we will continue to behave in self-destructive ways.

It is hardly news that another sign of America's dysfunctionality as a country can be seen in its huge numbers drug and alcohol addicts. My observations lead me to the conclusion that such addictions have less to do with chemical imbalances than many would have us believe; and that even genetic factors (which are undoubtedly real) can result in very different expressions, based on how one chooses to deal with them. Although there may well be a clear causal relationship between some addicts and their chemistry (and in some cases this can be traced to genetic factors), it is also likely that over decades of numbing ourselves with drugs and alcohol and non-nutritious foods, our body and brain chemistry changes to reflect the pattern. And this is, in all probability, not merely the result of what we are putting into our system, but of the mind-numbing effects of the habit pattern itself.

The reverse should be equally true. If we eliminate addictive and harmful substances from our body, several other things also happen.

For one, we substitute healthier habits—more nutritious foods, for example, or more exercise, or a better sleep schedule. Our exploration of how we react to things causes us to "wake up" and notice what is going on inside us, and then take action. If one action doesn't work, our internal feedback mechanism directs us toward more appropriate actions, until we find what works best for us.

Even more important is the concomitant awakening of our spirit. There is a synergy between our desire to get off the cycle of mind-numbing activities and substances, and the effects of the increased feedback that our bodies give us when improved habits free up our attention, thus allowing us to pay attention to ourselves. Our true heart's desire and soul's purpose begin to reveal themselves progressively when the desire to find them is sufficient, and when we make natural "lifestyle" changes to assist in directing us there. We then begin to glimpse the deep satisfaction that we have when our soul's desire becomes recognized and fulfilled.

The inherent joy of the authentic life does not subtract from its vulnerability, but it makes inauthenticity much less attractive (as well as easier to spot). That's why those who have gotten to that place of joy no longer are tempted to numb themselves out with food, drugs, entertainment, or any other means. Their principal high is the high of living out their deeper purpose. There are no prohibitions except the prohibition against numbing out. They flow with life's ups and downs, and these cycles are of secondary importance, because they have followed their inner compass.

Violent Anger

Rarely if ever do I see people who truly live their heart's desire express themselves in emotionally destructive ways towards others. When you live an authentic life, you experience a great sense of inner peace. From that inner peace come love, compassion, and full acceptance of others. There may be rare moments of anger even for such a person, but these moments are few and far between. The person that is socially and emotionally conscious sees these moments as opportunities to go inside and reflect on whether there is an imbalance, but it is in the context of the prevailing balance. Such an individual sees anger as an expression of something deeper—as emotional pain, as a reflection of some re-stimulated early childhood wound, or perhaps a reflection of disowned material in one's psyche. For most people, the biggest piece of disowned material is the soul's desire for realization of itself. Rarely does such a person externalize their anger or frustration. Instead he or she will recognize it for what it is, release it, and return quickly to equanimity, a balance borne out of understanding and natural compassion.

By way of contrast, those who are enamored with power, prestige and ambition for themselves tend to be consistently angry toward events and people around them. When their efforts to persuade or to control others don't produce a desired immediate effect, they will direct their anger toward the person or people who they believe are the cause, rarely realizing that the cause is their own desire for power itself, or unexamined and disowned aspects of their own inner world. Equally as likely, it is caused by lack of deep fulfillment, a deep soul wound that has not been healed.

Did you ever notice that people who seem to control others out-wardly have an enormous fear of being out of control? Did you ever notice that the people who brag about their abilities are the ones that feel the most insecure? It is because of their inner dis-ease that anger, control, and manipulation are used as unconscious strategies to tempo-rarily heal a much bigger and more enduring wound—the experience of being unfulfilled at the deepest level of existence.

It took me a while, but eventually I could see that I was most angry with my son when my life was not going the way of my ambitions. If I was not earning enough money or I had not done a consulting job as successfully as I had hoped, deep down I was hurting inside. My sense of self was so tied to outer success that when outer success momen-tarily eluded me I would get all wound up. Naturally, in such a state I would get upset easily, and my son was often the unwitting target. When I felt out of control, I would often unconsciously direct my rage toward him—to try to mold him into the man I wanted him to become. All this eluded me temporarily for he, of course, did things that were worthy of my upset. It's not the fact of the upset that came to trouble me. It was the strength of it, a strength born of my own insecurity and a strength he did not deserve to have directed at him. The invitations from my wife to notice what I was doing were eventually heeded, but not before some emotional pain was inflicted on my son.

By the time my son was still in his teens, something magical began to happen. I began to notice that the more I lived consistent with my soul's desire, the gentler I became. And the more I felt in complete alignment with my soul, living my heart's desire, the more spacious I became in relationship not only to my son, but to all people. Love and respect replaced judgment and anger, and my son and I were the beneficiaries.

I still get frustrated and even a little angry with him from time to time, and he still does things that are worthy of at least some response—leaving things lying around without awareness of the effect on me or others, failing to do things he promises—but I offer more gentle remonstrations than unconscious outbursts of anger, expressing my own deeper vulnerable feelings of hurt when he does certain things. He often receives these communications with tenderness and genuine remorse. Equally as important, I remember the self-centered nature of my own teenage years and have begun to recognize the natural cycle that this represents. Much like the "terrible twos," there are times when the psyche needs to be more focused on itself, and rather than rail against it, I have learned to accept the larger wisdom of my son's and all teenagers' needs to be self-oriented. It is in many ways a necessary step to developing a strong emotional self.

All the habits or choices I had exhibited, and the habits and choices exhibited by others (even, or especially, the more violent and dysfunctional ones), are reflections of a deep sense of un-ease that is ultimately the biggest indicator of an inauthentic life. Purely and simply, people who live a full and authentic life are at ease within themselves and therefore experience life in a natural flow. Those that are not leading the life of their heart's desire are constantly nervous, worried, or anxious. They have difficulty trusting life. They are wound tightly and vibrate at an unnatural level. They are constantly on the go, having to fill up their life with activity—or they are lethargic and withdrawn. Either way, they are unwilling to face their own inner condition of dis-ease.

An Exercise

Consider the possibility that any choice in life that takes you away from your natural state of health is a message to you that something is off. We may not know what it is and we may have numbed ourselves seeing the truth, but consider it as a possibility. Now, without shame or self-judgment, list in your journal all of the ways you numb yourself out or take things into your body that are not healthy. They can be foods you eat, watching too much TV, taking too much alcohol, too-frequent use of recreational drugs, or whatever else comes to mind.

Now look at this list as a whole and see if you can describe the consequences of these choices. Again without judgment or shame, acknowledge the consequences in terms of what you must be feeling as a result of these habits. Write down the consequences in your journal.

These habits and these consequences can be seen in many ways. But I want you to consider that they are a message to you. Underneath it all is an ache, a desire, a crying out for you to follow your deeper muse. We may not know what it is, but somewhere, deep in our bodies, we know we've turned away from something so fundamental that we can no longer see it through the cloud of our habits or our numbness. Be open to any notions, intuitions, or messages about this deeper self and deeper purpose that have been ignored or even forgotten through the habit of self-numbing—and write down your discoveries. If nothing comes up, at least hold open the possibility that it may come later.

A Balanced Stance

Those who follow their own inner guidance system feel centered and balanced. Our way of speaking and the energy behind it reveal our state of balance or imbalance. Whenever we push too hard, or withhold an important communication, we are out of balance. Whenever our speaking is designed for any purpose other than the pure expression that wants to be spoken, we are in a state of imbalance. We speak sometimes to break silence. We speak sometimes out of our own discomfort. We speak sometimes to try to impress others. We speak sometimes in ways designed to protect others. We speak to appease people's concerns. We speak to protect ourselves. We speak because we are narcissistically enamored with our own talk. None of these ways of speaking appears balanced to me.

Most of our speaking does not add true value. Imagine you have a bank account where, instead of money, "goodwill coins" are kept. The more coins in the bank account, the more you are able to positively influence others and are welcomed in community. Every time you speak, you either add coins to your goodwill bank account or spend them. When you speak, for any reason, you are either adding or subtracting goodwill coins. When you speak from your heart, in a wholehearted way, you are, in effect, adding coins to your "influence" bank account. When you don't speak from your heart—when your speaking is tainted with impure motivations and designs to control or avoid—you lose coins. How rich is your goodwill bank account?

Recently I sought to hire a marketing strategy consultant to help me market my previous book. Very early on, we had a hiccup in our relationship. It started when I blurted out something about our work together that did not sit well with the consultant. Although I was quite pleased with her work, the way it came out suggested the opposite. In other words, I spent some goodwill coins with her. And because our relationship was nascent, I didn't have many such coins to spend. I could tell almost immediately that she was starting to consider that perhaps she did not want to work with me. I wasn't sure what had put her off; I just knew I had, and asked her if this was true.

She beautifully raised the issue of how I came across, and as I listened to her concerns with an open heart, her goodwill bank account increased through the way she spoke to me. Mine, in turn, started to earn back coins by the way I listened and honored her feelings. Our relationship was quickly repaired and even enhanced, knowing we are able to discuss difficult issues in a humanly caring way.

There is an image I often use to check whether I am coming from an inner stance of authenticity and solidity. It is an image of my body leaning. When I am not feeling centered and confident, either I lean too far forward (pushy), or lean too far back (apologetic or avoiding).

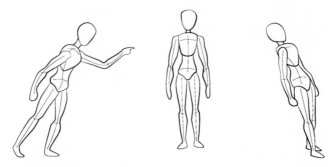

	Pushy or Aggressive	Centered and Confident	Fearful and Withheld
Thoughts	• I am worried • I am needy • I am concerned	• I am fine as I am • I am capable • I trust me and the situation	• I don't deserve this • I am not capable
Emotions	• Anxious • Unsettled • Insecure	• Safe • Confident • Secure	• Self-defeated • Unworthy • Fearful • Insecure
Behaviors	• Attacking • Blaming • Over-confronting	• Assertive • Inquisitive • Direct and compassionate	• Pulling back • Avoiding • Apologetic • Overly yielding
Outcomes	• Others reacting • Push back • Resistance • Resentment	• Change • Positive movement • Clear communication	• Little movement • Tentativeness • Disappointment

Figure 3: Different Stances

It is not so much that I am leaning physically; I am leaning energetically. When we lean forward too far, we are trying to exert power or control over others, and as a result they defend themselves or react to our exertion. Our message suffers when we force people to react to our aggressiveness, and they in turn become defensive or shut-down, so the message is not properly received. Instead they feel diminished and hurt, with little space to be themselves.

When we lean too far backwards, we are diminishing ourselves. We are giving away our power and in so doing, we shrink. We give away our power often in subtle and not-so-subtle ways. We give away power by acting in self-deprecating ways. We give it away by withdrawing or withholding our true feelings. We give it away through passivity. And we give it away be being overly apologetic for our actions especially when our actions were simply full expression of ourselves. When we lean too much in either direction, we are not coming from a solid stance within ourselves. The natural angle of authenticity is upright, centered, grounded, and true. However, it is best not to get caught up in or obsessed with your body posture. The angle of leaning is often a physical sign of energetic processes; ultimately, it is the energetic processes that should be of interest. It is most important to remember that when we are upright, living from our soul, we respond to life instead of react energeticly.

An Exercise

Using the model above, draw in your journal how you tend to lean in life. Do you tend to lean forward, taking an aggressive stance? Do you lean backward, so often yielding to others and disconnecting from your own truth? As you draw in your journal, see if you can feel in your body what it feels like to take that stance. Allow yourself to feel it as viscerally as you can. That bodily sense will create a powerful impression for you, far more than just the drawn picture.

If you are like most, different situations bring out different stances. Feel free to reflect in a more differentiated way about your patterns. Under what circumstances are forward-leaning or backward-leaning stances evoked in you?

For the next week or so, begin to notice the leaning stances you take when you interact with others, and how those stances might reflect certain feelings you are having. Also note how others receive you, and the role your leaning stance may play in this. As soon as practical after such an interaction, take a moment to reflect on the meaning of your forward-leaning or backward-leaning stance, using the guided process that follows. You may wish to repeat this exercise as often as is useful, gaining more information with repeated self-observation. Write some of your thoughts in your journal as you go.

As you write, consider what your surface thoughts and feelings were. What were the issues or challenges you were facing in this interaction? Were you reacting in a certain way to things the other person(s) said or did? Then consider what might have been the deeper impulses, needs, or feelings that lie underneath the surface. If you were leaning forward, the anger and demand that show up on the surface often mark a feeling of threat, loss, or fear. See if you can access those or identify what is truly there. Likewise, if you were leaning backward, your submissive or recessed stance may also be masking terror, loss, or fear—as well as insecurity or self-recrimination. (Whereas forward-leaning may signify an aggressive counter-reaction to the hidden underlying emotions, backward-leaning may signify a more passive reaction.) Write down your thoughts to these possibilities in your journal.

Remember that people respond differently to the same situation. Realize that your response and reaction is one you chose, and is not the one everyone would choose in the same circumstance.

Now imagine what it would be like to have responded in an upright stance—to have expressed yourself cleanly and effectively.

Imagine yourself speaking your truth, owning it, and offering it to another without either hesitation or aggressiveness. What would have been your thoughts and feelings had you remained upright? What would you have said? What would it have felt like to speak your truth cleanly? How might others have responded? Be sure to ask and answer these questions in sequence as expressed here. Write down your answers to these questions in your journal.

This is simply a practice ground. If you feel up to it, you may want to consider going back to a recent interaction and trying it out differently. While there are no guarantees, consider trying it and seeing what transpires. Whether you do it actually or imagine it, you are on your way to experiencing life from a more solid place. This is your inner compass at play. It is the essential ingredient to inner freedom.

Having established the philosophy and experience of following your inner compass, we will now turn to the essence of our exploration. We will wonder together how we can embrace ourselves fully and live authentically. We will enter into the "how to's" of living the life we were meant to live, stripping away the layers of the onion of our psyche, and eventually finding our inner core. And I will continue to offer exercises throughout each chapter, each designed not just to gain awareness, but to experience that more natural state of being.

CHAPTER FOUR

THE FIVE PROMISES

*"If you hear a voice within you saying, 'You are not a painter,'
then by all means paint… and that voice will be silenced."*

— Vincent Van Gogh

The Five Promises I introduce here (and elaborate upon in the following five chapters) have proven themselves in my work to be a very useful structure within which authenticity can be experienced. Each promise builds upon the prior one. Keep in mind that these are promises you are making to yourself, and that the reason you are making them is to be authentic to yourself—not to be perfect. Authenticity itself is always a work in progress; it is not a state one arrives at once and for all. These promises are useful insofar as they produce results in your life. The only "consequences" for non-fulfillment are those given by life itself. This is about liberating your spirit, not about burdening yourself with rules, injunctions, or guilt.

These are the five promises:

1. Let Go of the Shackles that Bind You.

You cannot live your own life until you are willing to break free of three primary forces—your ego, your cultural environment, and your fear. Each of these is present for a reason.

The ego is there to protect you and to help you assert your own independence. It is not there to take over your whole being or to control others. When it does, you experience a life disconnected from the fruits of deep relationship.

The culture is there to allow for a sense of community and for ease of interaction. It is not there to dictate to you how to live your life; if it does it is because you have let it.

Your fear is there to protect you—to be sure you don't make decisions that are risky or foolish. Fear keeps you alert to potential danger. Unfortunately for many, the difference between perceived danger and actual danger is quite difficult to discern. As a result fear, or rather the tendency to live from your fear, can also constrict and bind you. For many, letting go of the binding effects of the fear becomes a crucial step toward freedom.

2. Live with passion, consistent with your purpose.

Few of us know our purpose. Few even seek to find it. Our purpose is why we are on this earth—how we are meant to serve. To find our purpose requires that we be open to the possibility that each of us has a unique gift, something the world needs. Once we discover this gift (a challenge for many in itself), to lead a fulfilling life means that we express and live this purpose fully, without reservation. How it manifests is less important than that it does. This is often the hardest part, for it may well require a leap of faith and a willingness to buck the trend of societal expectations.

3. Live in full integrity. We are mind, body, and spirit.

When our thoughts, feelings and actions are all aligned, consistent with our principles, we are living an integrated life. Integration produces integrity. People who live in full integrity live a life of clarity and ease. They are in tune with their inner compass; therefore they are not obsessively focusing on others (or on the culturally-implanted "voices" in their own head) to decide what to do or say, or how to act. They are unencumbered by the nervous twitches, second guesses, and harsh self-reprimands that so many of us go through life with. They flow in life freely and easily.

4. Find and speak your truth.

It is only rarely that most of us know fully what is true for us. Even when we do, there are many truths we are hesitant to speak. All of this suggests aspects of ourselves that we don't feel good about or confident of—and that we are overly focused in on what others will think, and afraid of their rejection. Our self-judgment and even shame keeps us from expressing our deepest truths. We spend much of our life editing ourselves, hoping we are not fully seen. Each time we tell our truth, we affirm who we are and stand tall in our own hearts. Each time we elect to not tell our truth, we make ourselves small.

5. Remember that you are already connected to everyone and everything.

Remembering that you are already imbued with divine love and connected to all and everything is the fifth and final promise we need to make. It is not a promise to connect, for the connection is already there. It is a promise to remember. In coming from the presumption of connectedness, our connections deepen, even as our neurotic and fearful focus on others lessens. Too often we forget this universal connectedness. Instead, we live from and within a separated sense of self and in so doing, our natural reflex is to protect ourselves from these imaginary threats.

These five promises offer levels of satisfaction and fulfillment that we can scarcely imagine until we are in that authentic place. They are at the core of what it means to live a fully embodied life. Each promise builds upon the preceding one. The first step is to choose soul over a life defined by others. Once the choice is made, it requires that you get in touch with your deeper purpose (unless you are among the few who are already in touch with it). From this, you need to know and live your truth, and fully express yourself in an integrated way. Feeling solid inside, you naturally connect to others, and honor and invite others to connect to themselves.

The next five chapters expand on these steps and speak directly to what each promise means and what it requires. Please read these chapters in the spirit of inquiry. What I'm presenting here is born out of my own process and experience in guiding countless others. But ultimately, your own experience in these matters is more important than mine. What is important is that you find your own way to live your life and purpose with authenticity and passion. These five promises have proven especially helpful to me and to those I've worked with. I encourage you to try them, but ultimately you are invited to do what is most helpful to yourself.

CHAPTER FIVE

LET GO OF THE SHACKLES

*"Everything can be taken from a person but one thing: the last
of the human freedoms — to choose one's attitude in any
given set of circumstances, to choose one's own way."*

– Viktor Frankl

There once was a man who woke up one day only to discover he was trapped in a 10' x 10' room, with no windows and only one door. In the room was nothing but a wooden chair on which he sat—and an overwhelming feeling of despair, dread, and emptiness. Outside of the room was the rich fullness of life, replete with love, family, friends, purposeful work, and all the successes and failures, joys and despairs that are prerequisites for growth and an authentic life.

He recalled that during the night he had been abducted by a group of dangerous men who had informed him that he had to live the rest of his life in this room. They would feed him enough food to survive, but if he ever tried to escape, he would be shot and killed immediately. He was told that they stood outside the door day and night with machine guns ready to fire.

The man struggled in his mind. Was his memory true? Was the threat real, or was his mind playing a trick on him? Was he destined to live trapped in this room for the rest of his life? Would the mere possibility of living a free, fulfilling life make escape worth the tremendous risk? Was there a way out that he could not think of? Could he avoid the bullets? The decision was wrenching and he sat frozen, unable to move.

This story is a metaphor for our lives. Too often we live in a room that is empty—and we have been there so long that we take it as our given, unchangeable reality. Some part of us, following the dictates of our internalized messages from family and society, has abducted our soul and left us in this "place," devoid of passion and purpose. Outside of the room is the potential for a splendid life filled with freedom. There are dangers outside but you can only experience the fullness of life if you walk through the door. The problem is you can't say what might await you there; you can't say how your present life and identity might be threatened. And you won't know without risking that sense of certainty and stability that you now have. Our "inner abductors" tell us not to leave—that if we do, we might face ridicule and rejection from others. Our inner abductors "protect" us from this possibility and at the same time prevent us from living a full life. To live a full life requires that we let go of the shackles that bind us—that we strip away that which holds us back.

Michelangelo was once asked how he was able to sculpt his great masterpiece, David. His response is well known but worth repeating, as it expresses the visionary aspect of creativity so well:

"In every block of marble I see a statue as plain as though it stood before me, shaped and perfect in attitude and action. I have only to hew away the rough walls that imprison the lovely apparition to reveal it to the other eyes as mine see it."

—Michelangelo

The "rough walls" Michelangelo describes are a good metaphor for the trappings of inauthenticity that form a crust around our true self. Our goal should be to have the sensitivity of a great artist and be attuned to the life that lies behind these superficial trappings—a life and reality of which we are often completely unaware.

The first and most important of the promises we must make to ourselves is to break free of the forces that keep us from being authentically who we are. This may be the most difficult promise to realize, because these forces seem to be who we are. They are the "drama on the screen" that is so entrancing that we don't realize (or too often forget) that our true identity lies elsewhere. Yet, most often, we don't enjoy this drama; in fact, most of the time we find it suffocating without really knowing why. And so we remain trapped within a room of our own making.

Let's review the three forces that together conspire to bind us and keep us from living a fully realized life, which I introduced briefly in the previous chapter. The first is our ego, which is designed to protect a very narrow and limited view of who we are. The second is our environment, which includes the culture in which we are immersed; this acts as a massive weight, shaping the choices we allow. The third is our fears—often masquerading as anger, boredom, avoidance, or our continual need to "escape" reality—which constrict and confine us. Although these forces are really a part of a single tapestry, in order to better understand how they work, we will separate them in our discussion. This will give us a practical understanding of how we can chisel away these binding influences on our life.

Our Ego

Too often, our ego is seen as a problem—to be fixed or eradicated. But I believe it has an important function in our inner landscape—to protect us and to drive us to strive—and it needs to be strong and healthy. A strong and healthy ego protects us by helping us know our beliefs, our views, our needs, and what our body desires. Without an inner protector we would put ourselves in harm's way. With a strong ego, we can more easily ask for and get what we want and need in life. Without an ego, we would likely not move or reach or strive.

A strong ego is also the impetus that drives us to succeed or to seek fulfillment, even though it may be confused about where fulfillment ultimately comes from. To want to be fulfilled, to strive to better ourselves, is often an ego-driven desire, especially at first. Ego often propels our ambition and aspirations and gets us going. It helps us by imagining a more fulfilled life than the one we have, and it prompts us to go after it. Ironically, in order to finally arrive at deep and enduring fulfillment, we need to cast off the ego as our driving force.

Interestingly, a strong ego and a big ego are not the same. In many ways, they are the opposite. When we feel insecure inside and don't feel a strong sense of self, we have a need to boast—to prove to others how strong we are. This is often an affliction in male culture. When we say someone has a big ego, we mean he is boasting, bragging, trying to prove to others how wonderful he is. If he had no need to prove something—if his wonderful state of being were truly realized—then he would feel no need to boast. People with strong egos tend, therefore, to be quite unassuming, with little need for the spotlight.

An Exercise

Your ego has driven you to excel, to accomplish things, and to ensure certain parts of your life work. Assuming a part of your ego is healthy, how has it served you? List at least 5 ways in your journal.

The Problem With Our Ego

The problem with the ego is not that it exists, but that it too often takes over our lives in ways that are not healthy. Too often, the ego rules the roost where our inner lives are concerned. When it takes over, we are seen as a person who only cares about himself or herself, and decisions are made based on a perceived narrow self-interest. However, the ego's choices often do not coincide with our true interests, because our ego fails to understand our true nature.

Our egos have little to no ability to see reality. Out of a sense of self-protection our ego creates a dramatic story of what is going on. "She made me do it." "He's trying to hurt me." "You're punishing me with your words." "You don't want me to be strong." "You're doing that just to get me."

I recently had an experience that illustrates this point well. I was driving down the highway late at night when, after passing a car, the driver kept flashing his brights at me. It was as if he was saying, "Don't you pass me, you _____." Then, to add insult to injury, he began tailing me, staying uncomfortably close to me as he kept flashing his brights. I raced away to avoid this annoying driver only to be faced with another who did the same thing. I started to have images of being terrorized. I decided to exit, but the second car followed, continuing to flash his brights. I slowed down, realizing I had to face my fear, and as the car pulled next to me, I rolled down my window and with aggression in my voice said, "what the hell are you doing?" The driver rolled down his window and said, "Hey, your lights are off."

We have no access to reality through the ego, for all it can see is the ways the world might be threatening us. To the extent its job is to protect us it must be ever vigilant, trolling for and suspecting others of doing things that might hurt. Our ego has no ability to see love or feel love, to see compassion or feel compassion, to see connection or feel connection, for that is not its job. As a result it cannot see the divine that is inside us and ever-present.

One simple and profound way of thinking about the ego is that it is our automatic brain. In the face of physical or psychological threat, the ego, when given free rein, has certain predetermined and "primitive" sets of reactions that are often not based on the truest or wisest assessments of things—and never reflect our deep soul. Most of the threats we experience are psychological in nature—in fact, they are of our own making. The ego's perception of threat is born out of an interpretation that is often inaccurate. We attribute to people motives that are more often than not a reflection of our own projection, fueled by our ego driven fear.

- Sally steps forward during a meeting and raises a tough issue. Her intention is to invite dialogue, but John feels exposed by her action and believes she's out to get him.

- Ben, a teenager, gets involved with his friends and decides on the spur of the moment to go to a movie with them, forgetting to mow the lawn as he had promised. Joe, his father, who had an especially tough week, feels burdened by his work with no end in sight, and from that sense of overload believes his son just doesn't care and yells at him.

- Jeff feels that the kindest thing he could do for his wife, Sandra, is to give her room to be alone and makes some plans with his best friend to watch the big game at the bar. He would actually prefer to be with her but senses she needs some space. Sandra feels abandoned by Jeff even though she does need some time for herself, because it appears as if Jeff was only thinking about himself. Jeff had simply failed to tell her the kind thought that was behind his decision. When confronted by her, Jeff at last explains, but Sandra doesn't believe it is true. Now that he has to react to her, he sounds defensive (an ego under attack that is looking out for itself) and is therefore not believable.

The belief of threat causes judgment and then outbursts of anger, upset, and frustration. These are automatic behaviors and rarely expressions of our deep soul. Witness how you feel when you react, as if under siege. Notice the forward angle of your leaning, as if to attack or defend. These are clues that you are in reaction.

An Exercise

Think about the last three or four times you were in reaction to another or judged another. Reactions or judgments are ego-protective mechanisms. By reactions, I mean a feeling of rejecting another, getting angry with another, or feeling repulsed in some way. By judgment, I mean that you are looking at that person as wrong, bad, or not okay. Almost always reactions and judgments are in response to some kind of threat. Note that typically reactions have judgments embedded in them. List each incident and then on the left side of your journal, write the judgment or reaction you felt. On the right side, write what you sense may be the threat that may be behind or underneath the reaction or judgment. After writing, see if you can detect any meaningful patterns in what you react to, how you react, and the underlying threats that you experience.

In my view, A response is different from a reaction. A response is driven by an inner clarity and is not offered as a demand. It is guided by an awareness of and living from a sense of our own soul and divinity. It is solid, grounded, thought-out and thought-through. Or it is sensed or intuited; it comes from a deeper place of inner knowing. (Often it is a combination of these, although either thinking or sensing/intuiting may predominate.) In contrast with a reaction, a response can be a simple request, an expression of one's desire, or a simple, heartfelt feeling. It can be straightforward and direct, or gentle and suggestive. Notice the angle of your body when you offer a response. It is typically upright and invites response rather than reaction in return. The stronger we are inside ourselves, the less we experience psychological threats, and the less our ego takes over.

By choosing to respond from a deeper place, we have access to our natural wisdom. Wisdom is guided by a sense of connection to all and everything. Wisdom is able to take into account our own needs, the needs of others, and the contexts in which we operate. Wisdom is able to make choices that meet the needs of all, including our self. Our ego can only focus on our own needs, often to the exclusion of or in conflict with others. Our ego is what drives us to war and to every kind of strife we see on the interpersonal, political, and international stage.

The Bind of our Environment

In so many ways, we are social beings. The whole field of sociology was born out of that realization. Sociology is the study of social forces, and they are far more powerful than we give them credit. In the words of my old professor, they have a facticity. The power of the crowd (or of "others") weighs heavy on our psyche and has a powerful control over what choices we make, often quite unconsciously. One need not go too far to understand this. Just notice how people behave differently in different societies. Each one has its unwritten rules. Witness the different ways a friend might be greeted when unexpectedly met while walking down the street. In Sweden, the friends might shake hands and greet each other with a cool smile. In Italy, they'd offer a full-body embrace. In Los Angeles, it might be an air kiss coupled with a sound that sounds like "mwa." In France, it might be a light kiss on each cheek. No one told any of these people the rules of greeting. They just picked it up, having observed others in social settings, and in no time it required as little thought as the language we speak.

I had the chance to witness the powerful and unconscious force of our environment recently while at a baseball game with my daughter. I don't particularly enjoy baseball but my eight-year-old daughter was showing signs of being interested in softball, so I thought I'd take her to a game as a way of encouraging her nascent interest.

As is traditional at American sports just before the game began, we all stood up and put our hands on our hearts as the national anthem was sung. Being someone who enjoys singing and, for whatever reason, enjoys this particular song, I sang it out loud while all around us, people were silent. Clearly I was alone, but that didn't bother me. I sang, happily. As I did, my daughter glowered at me and then kicked my leg. Initially, I had no idea why she was doing that, but clearly it caught my attention. I continued to sing nonetheless, not wanting to be interrupted. She kicked again, and then again, and then she pushed me.

"What?" I asked, in a playful tone, curious about what was so urgent. Her eyes darted all around us and then she frowned. "What?" I asked again.

"You're embarrassing me," she blurted out. "Stop singing!"

"Why?" I asked, curious at the intensity of her feelings.

"You-are-embarrassing-me," she said, assertively emphasizing each word as if it deserved its own punctuation.

"Because I'm singing and no one else is?" I replied, finally understanding fully what was happening.

"Duh," she replied, rolling her eyes.

Now to appreciate this moment, you need to realize that both my ex-wife and I have encouraged our children to express themselves fully and freely. Neither of us is a "sameness" thinker and we encourage our children to be whoever they want to be. In other words, they were never taught by us to follow the crowd; quite the opposite. Somehow, though, my daughter learned that one was supposed to go along with the crowd. Was it an innate desire or was it taught? If taught, it wasn't in our family. I think it is perhaps both. I think somehow we are wired for connection. We seek to identify with groups. Many people join clubs for camaraderie. We put flags out on our doorstep marking our proud association with our country. We work at organizations and learn their particular rules and customs. We gain pleasure and comfort in knowing we are a part of something. Rare indeed is the person that really goes it alone in life.

It's as if we have a deep, innate desire to be in community. At the same time, we learn, especially in our school system, to follow the rules of our society. Our teachers, out of an obligation to teach those rules and out of a need to create a semblance of order out of an especially unruly class of citizens known as children, place great emphasis of following the basic rules of society and of the classroom. As a result, my daughter has learned to be a "sameness" thinker—to go with the crowd. Under the weight of such a force, she and others like her learn how to be proper, to be polite, and do the right thing where right is defined by the culture or environment in which we live. And it all happens quite unconsciously. And as a result, we do not become independent thinkers, standing on our own two feet. To become so requires enormous confidence in oneself, and few seem to have it.

Those that do break out of the mold are often ostracized, for the culture tends to try to spit out those that don't conform.

- Galileo Galilei, was tried by the Inquisition, found guilty of heresy and sentenced to house arrest for the rest of his life by the church for daring to try to prove Copernicus's theory that the earth revolves around the sun and not the other way around.

- Einstein was ridiculed for his theory of relativity that ran counter to the prevailing views of science at the time.

- In the mid 1960s Dick Fosbury dared to defy the notion that the best way to jump over a high bar was forward or sideways, as had been the prevailing practice, by jumping backwards. His peers laughed at his gangly gait, until he won the gold medal for high jumping at the Olympics in 1968 and simultaneously broke the Olympic record. Now, what used to be called the "Fosbury Flop" is simply called, "high jumping."

In each of the reactions to the culture-defying act we can see the power of the culture to bounder its quarry. If you've ever wondered about the power of the environment to shape our lives and its potential coercive effect, you need look no further than three fascinating and even disturbing social psychological experiments. Remember what Peter Berger said about social facticity as you read these.

Administering Shocks

In one famous study conducted in 1961 by Stanley Milgram, 40 volunteer subjects (recruited via ads) were given the role of teacher while another individual—who was introduced by the experimenter as another subject but was actually, unbeknownst to the subjects, a confederate, or research partner who acts the part—played the role of student. In each experiment, involving "teacher" and "student", the "student" was given a set of word pairings to memorize and then repeat back upon cue. If the "student" got the answer wrong, the "teacher" was instructed by the researcher to deliver an electric shock to the "student" to punish them for the inaccurate answer. The "shocks" were delivered by pressing a button on a panel. The panel has buttons with descriptors in 40 increments, from mild to the highest levels, labeled "Extreme Intense shock," "Danger, Severe Shock," and the final level marked as "XXX", implying an ominous level of pain. While the "student" did not actually ever experience a shock, he acted as if he did. To add weight to the proceedings, the researchers carried themselves with great authority, dressing like scientists and speaking with great conviction about the importance of what was being researched,

At first, the subjects willingly administered the shocks, but they were instructed that for each successive incorrect answer, they were to increase the intensity, clearly marked on a panel. As the shocks seemed to be more and more painful as evidenced by the cries from the "learner" (who was in a separate room but could be heard by the teacher), subjects naturally started to hesitate, but most continued, feeling the weight of the authority of the researchers and their admonitions to go on with the experiment. As the "pain" worsened to the point where the "student"-subject was writhing, screaming, and demanding to be released from the experiment, the subjects all told the researchers they wanted nothing more to do with this for they didn't want to inflict such pain. The researchers admonished the subjects ever more strongly that this is an important study and that they agreed to participate so they must continue. In spite of the growing consternation and extreme feelings of tension on the part of many subjects, two-thirds of the subjects continued to administer shocks to the highest, excruciatingly painful level, and none of the participants quit the experiment even when the learner screamed out several times that he had heart trouble.

Prior to the completion of this study, experts thought only a very small percentage of subjects who were truly psychopathic (believed to be no more than 1 to 3 percent) would carry through with the shocks to the end; in fact, 65% did. Interestingly, the study has been replicated on several subsequent occasions, and the results each time were similar (although differences were found between cultures).

Not Standing in One's Truth

In another famous study by Solomon Asch in 1955, subjects were recruited for a study of visual perception and asked to simply judge the relative size of three lines on a set of cards. Two lines in each card were the same length while one was slightly shorter or longer. The subjects were asked to identify the line that was of a different length. While making the determination alone, with no one else present, subjects made the correct call 99% of the time. However, when placed in groups with confederates who appeared to also be research subjects, and when those confederates made a very different determination than the one the subjects were virtually certain was correct, subjects not only consistently second-guessed their answer but offered up the incorrect answer 75% of the time. In other words, only 25% would stick to their guns in the face of opposing viewpoints. The 75% who consistently changed their mind said that it was easier to go with the crowd, or that they really felt they must be wrong because of what they heard from the others.

We're All Prisoners of Our Roles

In a famous experiment known as the Stanford Prison Study conducted in 1971, Philip Zimbardo invited young adults (mostly college students and young citizens from middle to upper middle class backgrounds) to explore what it is like to be in prison—not only for inmates but for guards as well—with an eye to learning about the power of the crowd and of the roles one plays to shape behavior. The subjects, all of whom had volunteered to participate in the study, were randomly placed into two groups: "prison guards" and "prisoners." The "prisoners" were stripped of all belongings and had to live in a prison-simulated environment for many days. The "guards" were asked to administer a small set of rules to keep them there.

What transpired was both fascinating and disturbing as the mock "guards" and "prisoners" began to adopt behaviors that were very similar to those one would expect of real-life guard and prison populations. "Guards" seemed compelled to create a huge number of rules and became ever more intolerant, punitive, and even violent in their behavior against even the smallest of transgressions on the part of the mock prisoners. "Prisoners" became more and more rebellious and violently aggressive, in return inspiring even greater control mechanisms on the part of "guards." The social milieu in which each group lived together and the expectations that the roles seemed to imply reinforced these extreme opposing behavioral patterns with little to no prompting on the part of the researches who watched in awe as the drama unfolded.

What to Make of All of This

These are only a few of the studies that show, time and time again, the overwhelming power of perceived authority and social expectations to alter one's actions and opinions. Normal and healthy human beings will question their own ethics and adopt even violent behavior in order to meet the expectations of others, however absurd these expectations may seem. It's as if we as a human species would do almost anything to be part of the crowd. We are subject to a larger dynamic within which we unconsciously give up our own authority despite our bodies and our inner promptings telling us something is quite off here. Such is the facticity of our social environment, and it can be powerful indeed.

I've never forgotten that particular visit to the Ben Franklin Museum in Philadelphia as an eight- or nine-year-old boy. There was a wonderful exhibit devoted to Thomas Alva Edison, the great American inventor, who among other things invented the incandescent light bulb, the first viable radio, the phonograph, and the first commercially successful movie player, then known as the Vitascope. It wasn't the inventions that caught my eye, although they were quite impressive in and of themselves. What grabbed my attention were the quotes that were strewn among the exhibits. One in particular has stuck with me ever since. He said: "There is no extent to which a man will not go to avoid the full labor of thinking."

This avoidance of thinking is particularly true when it comes to questioning the precepts of our society. Like the water in which a fish swims, the paradigms that govern our lives are difficult to see, for they are ever-present. If they were suddenly to disappear, these paradigms would be much more obvious! But they feel so natural that we just don't think about them.

The Bind of Our Definition of Success

Perhaps the biggest and most difficult thing to break free of is our society's definition of success. It is the cause of a massive unconscious confusion concerning what constitutes a satisfying life. In this world, we chase after the illusion that satisfaction has to do with what we own as opposed to who we are. Let me explain how this happened.

Prior to the American Revolution, success in North America was defined largely in terms of right living or prevailing against challenging obstacles, rather than in material success. Early on, the Pilgrims and other voyagers to America were fueled by a desire to challenge the stronghold that the monarchy and aristocratic society had on the culture of Europe. People who came here to live were pioneers, seeking freedom of religious expression. Those that came to America would bow to no man (or woman) on the basis of what they owned or their lineage. The pioneering spirit, then, was the early defining quality of a successful life. When you add, however, abundant natural resources, a centralized banking system inspired by Alexander Hamilton's Federalist sensibilities, a belief that human beings were created to exert dominion over nature, and the capitalistic economic system where free enterprise reigns supreme, you have an elixir that was destined to produce an arc of economic success like none other in the history of the planet.

We Americans have enjoyed the riches of that combination of forces for all our lives and few question it. To this day, in the face of dwindling natural resources, global warming, and rampant population growth, we continue to believe it is our God-given right to enjoy the standard of living to which we have grown accustomed regardless of its long-term devastating consequences to Mother Earth. As a society, the current definition of success is the only one we seem to collectively know. It has been growing as a paradigm for a couple of centuries, and then got locked into place in the years after World War II when TV shows and advertisements depicted the good life in terms of material extravagances—a bigger house, a nicer car, and all the goodies that go along with economic success.

Our ego's desire for more and more was fueled and fashioned at an earlier time, and anyone born in the past 60-plus years has experienced an extraordinary imbalance between the trappings of the ego and the forces of soul and divinity that comprise our true nature. Ego has won out to such an extent that most people have no sense of any other way of being.

I recently walked past a homeless person sitting on a street in San Francisco on the way to a meeting, and witnessed a fascinating drama. Another homeless person came rushing forth and snapped his finger at the one sitting yelling, "Hey, go away. That's my spot!" They got into an argument, and the one who snapped his finger eventually won out, as the scorned homeless man walked away defeated. At that point the victor proudly perched himself at that exact spot.

His spot was his life raft. Never mind that it was not a house or a piece of property he owned. It represented his castle, giving him comfort, security, and a sense of belonging and maybe even continuity. Perhaps at a certain primitive level, this is what our ego "needs" to "survive." We will even go so far as to kill other people in order to hold onto our illusion of security. The difficulty is that when we define ourselves in terms of what we own rather than who we truly are (namely our essence and our goodness as human beings), we will hold on to these outer trappings for dear life.

Economic success has become the very definition of fulfillment, to the virtual exclusion of our connection to soul and divinity. This version of "success" has taken over our lives to the point that the thought of living more simply and therefore being in a right relationship to the Earth seems subversive. It seems to violate our right to dominion over the Earth and freedom from any limitations to our actions (even if those limitations improve the lot of others or help our society to function better). It appears that other countries are rapidly following suit, such as China, Russia and Brazil, wanting their turn to feed from our Earth's bountiful and yet dwindling trough. What is difficult for many people to see is that our very standard has embedded in it a set of assumptions which, when gone unquestioned, produce a never-ending slide toward the decay and eventual death of our planet. When other countries join the feeding frenzy, the process of destruction simply speeds up.

This particular pattern of not questioning came home to me powerfully during the presidential election of 2008, where Democrats and Republicans alike promised that their plan would do a better job than the opponents' plan for protecting the American way of life—as if the way we have been living were sacrosanct and sustainable. And can you blame them? We the people of the United States are hardly likely to vote for a candidate who says anything to the contrary. Our leaders are a reflection of ourselves. Even in the face of evidence of decay, we hold steady to our beliefs and don't question.

Such a pattern does not exist in our country alone. It is rife in almost every corner of the planet. As the "good life" of the U.S. is plastered all over the globe through television and the Internet, billions of others are exposed to and swept up by the illusion of the now-distorted version of the American Dream. And amidst this powerful force, it is extraordinarily difficult to rise above the masses and offer a truly different voice.

An Exercise

Think about a time when you felt compelled to go along with the crowd. You knew you felt differently than most, but you gave in and went with the crowd in order to not challenge others or in order to be safe. In your journal, write down the situation and what you did in that situation. For this, I recommend that you consider each situation and reflect in succession on each of the following:

1. The Situation:
2. What Some Deeper Part of Me Wanted to Do:
3. What I Chose to Do:
4. What I Gained:
5. What I Lost:

Material Success and True Satisfaction Are Not the Same

As I write these words, we finally appear to be at the end (we are told) of a huge economic downturn that has lasted over four years. With almost 10% of the adult working population out of work it was, without a doubt, the worst recession of most of our lives. Its weight was massive. Many people feel depressed and are in terror of what the future might bring. The process of trying to find a job only to be told time and time again none is available is truly depressing.

You may recall the friend I wrote about in the Introduction who had been on the brink of suicide. He and I talked about this recently, and the conversation tapped into a deeper truth of his plight. He discussed how much he bought the story of the American Dream and as a result, felt empty and ashamed of his failure to be a good provider. He is not a failure as a man and as a human being at all, for he exudes love and kindness wherever he goes. People are consistently touched deeply by his goodness. But that is how he has felt, and that is the point. His ego knows nothing else, and it has beaten him down. Thankfully, our exploration of these issues offered a glimmer of hope, not of reclaiming the possibility of financial riches, but of living a life from a deeper place than the one he, like most of us, has habitually and unconsciously adopted. Like others before him, he has the possibility of riding the waves of this enormous economic downturn without losing his sense of spirit. To do so requires a shift, not so much in the way we relate to the outer world, but in the way we relate to (and acknowledge) our inner world.

Abraham Maslow, were he viewing today's situation, might say that it is the result of our basic needs not being met—and that you can't get to self-esteem or become self-actualized (a term for living one's soul purpose) until the our needs for food, shelter, security and, love are met. And yet I have witnessed so many people who are not secure, who are unsure of what is next, who still seem to find grace within themselves and a consistent sense of joy. They may be out of work, and uncertain about where enough money will come from, but they are filled with love, inner peace, and gratitude.

There are very few people in the country who are starving to death. They are finding shelter where and when they can and making it through. What causes their depression is not the outer circumstances, which I admit are difficult for many, but the way they hold those circumstances. They are bereft, not from without but from within. In other words, people I know who are good with themselves and whose sense of self is located somewhere other than in material success seem to be fundamentally happy even amidst the mightiest of challenges, while those who are not good with themselves, who cannot find or follow their own inner muse, are often extraordinarily disheartened in the very same circumstances.

Interestingly, most of the legends and myths of times past warn us of the very type of plight we are in today, and they offer clear signs of our potential salvation. In traditions of European mythology, for example, our ego is often depicted as a dragon. The dragon is a powerful creature that breathes angry fire to anyone who dares to trespass and threaten its most precious quarry—its gold. Virgins are symbols of goodness, spirit, love and beauty. It is the hero's job to marry the virgin beauty (make love with soul and spirit) and to slay the dragon (overcome the ego). What if success had nothing to do with what I own or what I do, but instead with who I am inside and how I conduct myself in the world of others?

To live a fulfilling life requires we break away from the shackles of our society that dictate and define who we are supposed to be—how we're supposed to think and how we're supposed to act. It means becoming neither a "sameness" thinker (or conformist) nor a "difference" thinker (or contrarian). It means becoming your own thinker, which means accessing the deepest level of who you are.

The Taboo Against Knowing Who You Are

There is, in our society, a taboo against knowing who we are. This taboo is not written. It is felt. You can feel the taboo when a person is reflective and someone says, "oh, she's too deep," or "you think too much about things." You can see the taboo when a child colors outside the lines and the teacher reminds him that good children color inside the lines. You can see the taboo when we are given the rulebook and told to follow. And most powerfully, you can see the taboo when someone expresses themselves counter to the prevailing norms and you can hear the whispers of disdain and judgment.

The culture that surrounds us is a powerful force, and it weighs heavily on the soul. It shapes much of how we think and how we express ourselves in the world. It keeps us from finding and living consistent with our core selves.

To understand the relationship between our core self and how we express ourselves through our cultural boundaries, let's return to the examination of the core self and look at some of the layers that are wrapped around us.

As explored earlier, we start with the core self, which is comprised of our soul and our divinity.

Figure 5-1: The First Layer of Human Being

Wrapped around that core self is our ego crust, that layer of individual need that mediates and often drives what we choose to do and how we relate to the world, especially when feeling stress or a sense of scarcity and mistrust in the world. The more unsafe and fragile we feel, the harder it is to penetrate this crust and experience our soul. It is both a powerful protective mechanism, designed to ensure we are safe, and (at the same time) a powerful barrier to experiencing the extraordinary sense of fulfillment that is available to us in living from our core.

I had a dream last night that my sister, Wendy, had been transformed and become this wonderful being, filled with love and light. I wondered inside my dream whether she had transformed or I had simply finally become open to seeing her true deepest nature. Through the challenges of our childhood with one another, filled with battles and anger, and the cold distance of our adulthood, perhaps I had not been able to see her inner beauty. She and I have related to each other ego to ego and have had difficulty seeing the beauty that lies deeper within. Throughout my life, my ego protection has been strong with her and hers with me. Perhaps as the crust around my ego begins to soften, something is finally emerging in me: my ability to see through her encrusted armor to the beautiful woman she has become, and perhaps always was.

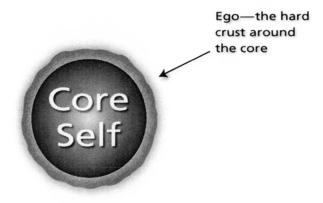

Figure 5-2: The Second Layer—The Ego Crust

At the next layer we find our personality. Interestingly, the word "personality" comes from the root word "persona," which in ancient Greek drama means "mask." In this vein, our personality can be understood as the mask that we show to the world. Being a mask, it is not as deep as the core self, and in most of us it tends to disguise the existence of the core self. It is what we consciously or unconsciously choose to show the world, and it is what the world sees or chooses to see—or, more specifically, what the world infers from what it sees.

There are many systems for understanding differences in personality. Among the more popular is the Myers-Briggs Type Indicator, which is largely derived from Carl Jung's original observations about differences among people. The Enneagram of personality is another such typology and one that I prefer, for it offers a deeper understanding of the patterns that cause the formation of our personalities.

While there are differences among personality typologies, they have a number of common assumptions. Central among them is that our personality represents ingrained patterns of behavior that have become a part of us. While individual behaviors will vary, the patterns often remain unchanged throughout adult life. By adulthood, our personality is deeply etched into our psyches. Some have argued that it is genetically baked into our personhood and should not be altered, for to do so would alter our "natural" state, causing angst, discomfort, and disease. Most psychologists believe that, to be healthy at the level of personality, it is better to understand and accept one's personality than to try to change it. That doesn't mean that our personality is rigid and can only be expressed in a certain way. Rather, most experts say, we can learn fluidity and flexibility and should strive to express our personality in more healthy and mature ways.

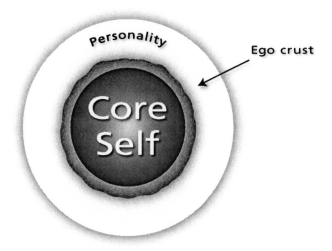

Figure 5-3: The Third Layer of Human Being

At the next layer of human experience are the cultural norms, expectations, and rules that weigh heavy on our lives. They are often unwritten, yet they tell us how to live and tell us what is deemed right or wrong. Over time, we gain great comfort in doing that with which we've become familiar and don't question its wisdom. Our brain gets used to these norms and expectations and prescriptions; they become so ingrained that we are no longer aware of what we believe and why.

I got a strong sense of this when I went to college at the University of Northern Colorado, located in Greeley, Colorado. Greeley is named after the great pioneer Horace Greeley, known for having coined the phrase "go west, young man." One of its other distinctive qualities is that the Mumford Feed Lots—where cattle were fed until their ultimate slaughter—were located there at the time.

When I first arrived at school, the stench from the feedlots was mighty. Interestingly, after about three or four days, all my fellow students and I became unaware of it. It receded into the background. Our brains and bodily chemistry were able to adapt to the toxic smell and ultimately became unaware of its existence. Even when we left for vacations and then returned, the smell was hardly detectable to our accustomed senses. The only time we became aware of it was when we were visited by out-of-towners who inevitably commented about the nasty odor upon their arrival. Typically I failed to warn people of this, for I had truly forgotten its existence.

Our culture in all of its forms, including its toxicity, has coexisted with our ego development in our childhood, at which time our earlier memories of a different world tend to recede or even disappear. Therefore, we never really question the norms that govern our lives; they are just "the way things are." They are background and are even invisible to us—or they are defended as objective truth, because we have no understanding of how they became our norms. Sometimes we may see our cultural assumptions more clearly when exposed to another culture that operates on different assumptions. Through this we get a glimpse that life as we've known it is not all that we believed it to be. We learn through different environments (or, more accurately, we have the potential to learn that perhaps our way is not the only way.

I heard an amusing story once that brings this point home in an amusing way. As the story goes, a girl watched her mother cutting off each end of the ham before placing it in the pan to be cooked. "Why do you do that," asked the inquisitive daughter.

"Oh, I don't know," came the mother's reply. "It's just the way it's done."

"But why is it done that way?" the girl persisted.

Rather than dismiss her daughter out of hand, the mother began to wonder about it herself and realized this is the way her mother had done it and she had never questioned it before. She called her mother up on the phone and asked, "Why did you always cut each end of the ham before placing it in the pan to be cooked?"

The grandmother in turn replied in much the same way the mother had done. "It's the way my mom did it and so I thought it was how it was done."

"But why?" queried the mother, now quite amused by the pattern that was clearly unfolding before her. The grandmother, curious about this, called her mother and the great grandmother laughed at the question. "We only had a small pan at the time and could not afford a bigger one. In order for the ham to fit into the small pan, I cut each end."

Over and over again, the environment presses on us and becomes a powerful mediator of our behavior. Our inner core and our personality have their own drive, but our true self gets filtered and often dampened by cultural expectations.

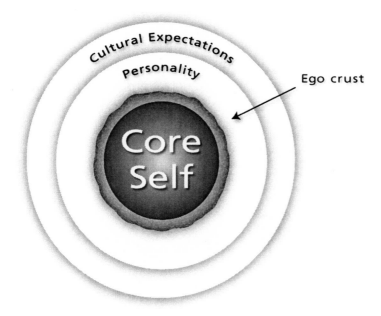

Figure 5-4: The Fourth Layer—Cultural Imperatives

At the outermost layer of human experience lies our behavior—the daily actions, decisions, and choices we make. Naturally, there are an infinite variety of behaviors one can exhibit, and they change, moment by moment. Sadly, though, while infinite varieties are possible, too often comparatively few are exhibited.

We do things because we are told, because those things are expected, because "that's the way it's done," not questioning the veracity of the choice. Our cultural expectations are a powerful mediator that shapes what we do and what gets expressed. And these expressions are rarely a reflection of our deepest calling and our deepest knowing. Human expression takes on a great variety, because much about each of us is unique, but that does not mean our own expression reflects our deepest self or our most creative potential. Indeed, our automatic behaviors tend to take on a bland sameness when our creativity is stifled by conformance to expectations.

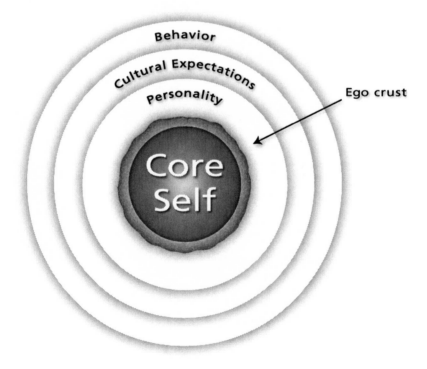

Figure 5-5: The Five Layers of Human Being

That is not to say that all of society is wrong or a problem. Much of society's dictates are wonderful and wise. Laws are often necessary and helpful. They protect us. They are nonetheless, based on rule by majority or by a kind of collective consensus, or are an expression of our collective unconscious, and are not necessarily designed with your soul in mind.

To break free and live a life guided by our own inner compass requires the direct and full commitment to follow our own inner muse and refuse to be dictated to by the conformist pressures of society. It requires that we let go. I am reminded of a story I once heard about surrender. There was a man who fell off a cliff and barely caught a protruding root of a tree, saving him temporarily from an untimely death. Hanging on the root for dear life, he yelled at the top of his lungs, "Help, help, is anyone there, help!" All of the sudden he heard a booming, echoing voice from above the clouds. "It is I, the Lord. If you want to be saved, you must let go." The man calls back, "Is there anyone else there?"

Willing to let go of the precepts that have guided our lives does not mean automatically rejecting or rebelling against them. That would not be a conscious choice at all, for then you are imprisoned in your own reactions. It means to question, and to wonder about the extent to which this choice is true for me. It means to have the inner compass of your soul, not culture's dictates, be the final mediator. In some cases, it may mean breaking away from your family your community, your church or temple, or your friends. Your soul may require this of you, and to be fulfilled in life requires following the attractiveness of your heart's desire and your soul's purpose.

The Bind of Fear

For some, it is not the culture and its weight that confines them; it is their inability to honor themselves. They spend so much time thinking about, caring about, and honoring others that they forget themselves. Their "self" or soul speaks in such hushed tones that they cannot hear it. Their inner compass is faint at best. In the rare moments they do gain access to its message, they fear heeding the call. As a result, they lack inner freedom.

The fear may feel quite justified, for to honor one's own muse may (one feels) mean conflicts with others or pushing them away. Such actions may seem intolerable to many, particularly those who find deep satisfaction in relationship to another. When one is directed so much by others and their needs, honoring oneself seems terrifying.

I have a friend, Samantha, who, along with her twin sister, is part of a complementary pair. Not uncommon among fraternal twins, they act like a hydraulic system, taking on characteristics that the other lacks. Samantha is quite gentle, amazingly able to sense what others need and to seek to find ways of meeting those needs. At the same time, she has enormous difficulty finding her own true voice. Her sister, in contrast, is quite dominant, facile in self-expression and equally facile in getting her needs met.

You can easily imagine that over the years, Samantha would take care of her sister in any of a number of ways. She would be happy for her sister's successes and appreciate her sister's ability to be out there. To be loving and giving seems natural to Samantha, baked into her from a young age and reinforced over the years.

Now, however, as a mature adult, Samantha is painfully aware that she doesn't know what she truly wants. She told me recently that she had a strong desire to write a book yet has no clue what to write about. I believe this desire to write is her soul aching to be expressed. The inability to know the book's content reflects her lack of awareness of who she is separate from her sister and separate from the world. In her growing-up years, to find and express herself fully would have risked the delicious cocoon that Samantha lived in where the more she gave, the more her sister felt comfortable. You can easily imagine that if Samantha tried to break free, the competition with her sister who had, for whatever reason, ample self-expression, might have been intolerable. Rather than risk that, my friend quietly subordinated and even subsumed herself.

While this is a rather clear-cut example, many people have similar fears—that if they broke free, they'd have to face some loss, and to face that would be intolerable. Sometimes it is the anticipated loss of love from members of one's family. Sometimes it is literally the loss of money, as in the case of wealthy parents who give money contingent upon the career choice of the child. Sometimes it is the fear of success, that shining beyond one's siblings or parents or community may lead to ostracism. Sometimes it is the fear of failure—to try and to fail feels intolerable.

Whatever it is, the person seeking an authentic life must break through or forever be bound in fear. They key is not to disown the fear or try to get rid of it, for neither works. The key is to find the proper relationship to the fear so that it does not own you.

An Exercise

I invite you to conduct the following step by step exercise as a way of sensing and feeling the barriers inside yourself to following your own inner compass.

Step One

Find a comfortable space where you can think for a while, undistracted and preferably at a place that supports you in thinking freely. It could be the woods, on a mountain, near a stream or brook, near the ocean, or simply in a room in your dwelling that feels life-giving.

Now sit comfortably and meditate for however long you need until you feel grounded and centered, open and free.

Now imagine living your life to the fullest, exactly the way you want it to be. Imagine freely all aspects of your life and what it would be like for you to be saying, doing, being exactly the way you want to be. This is a no-holds-barred exercise. Allow yourself to feel the full sense of expansive possibility, in which you are able to shape your life. What would your work be? With whom would you be working? What impact would you be having? How would you be living? Where? In what kind of dwelling? Who would you be relating to? Who would be your friends?

As you enter this realm of imagination, pay particular attention to how you're feeling. Notice the sense of expansion you feel.

At the same time, you may notice disbelief creeping into your awareness. Let it be there. Do not focus on it, just notice it for now and register that it exists.

Step Two

Now write down in your journal your imaginations of the inner freedom you could have.

Step Three

Now write down in your journal how it might feel to be in this life.

Step Four

In your journal, write down all the doubts that come up for you about being in this world. Write the judgments, the fears, and the self-inflicted boundaries that emerged for you in imagining this world. Often these doubts come in the form of beliefs, but not always. Sometimes they are fears or judgments. If you're not accustomed to examining your life in this way, I recommend you break down your doubts in the following arenas:

1. Beliefs I have that may prevent me from living this life:
2. Fears I would have to face to live this life:
3. Limiting judgments or boundaries I have about myself or others that might get in the way of living this life.

Write these doubts in a column on the left hand side of your journal, leaving plenty of room to the right. You will need that space for an additional piece of the exercise to be communicated later.

Step Five

Now consider the possibility that all of these beliefs, fears, and boundaries are ones you made up. They are the story you tell yourself when imagining your full life. If they are a story, is there an alternative story you might tell?

Next to each entry on the left hand column, write down the alternative story where your inner barriers are no longer present. For example, if your limiting belief is that "others will not support me," write down on the right hand column that "others would support me fully." Or you might write that "some will support and some will not. What matters is my own internal support."

Step Six

As a final step, look over your entries as a whole and ask yourself the question: What would need to shift for you to break free of the shackles of your own story—the story that is your life as you know it currently? Write down your answer in your journal.

Ultimately, to break away from the cultural shackles that bind you requires that you live an examined life. It requires that you question your own beliefs and the beliefs around you. Too often people don't know what they want, what they believe. They want what society says they should want. They believe without question. If I questioned things too much my parents would not love me, so better not to question.

If you are ready to question, to find your own true calling, read on, for the journey is not over. It has only just begun.

CHAPTER SIX

LIVING PASSIONATELY WITH PURPOSE

*"When you were born, you cried and the world rejoiced.
Live your life so that when you die, the world cries and you rejoice."*

– Cherokee Expression

You have a choice—to live your life based on the dictates of the society and culture that molded you, or to uncover your soul's purpose and follow it. In 1950, sociologist and educator David Riesman, in his groundbreaking book The Lonely Crowd,[11] offered an important distinction between two different types of people: those that are primarily outer-directed and those that are primarily inner-directed. He suggested that the people that are most satisfied in life are inner-directed.

Riesman's conclusion is correct as far as it goes. But, while being inner-directed is a necessary condition for satisfaction, it is not a sufficient one. Inner-directedness itself can come from either our soul or our ego. Many people spend much of their lives driven by their ego with no sense of connection to their soul and their divinity. They are inner-directed, to be sure, but it is a direction born out of protection. As a result, they are rarely fulfilled in the deepest sense.

David Whyte's poem, "Self Portrait," published in his collection, Fire in the Rain, points to what it is like to be directed from one's soul.

It doesn't interest me if there is one God or many gods.

I want to know if you belong or feel abandoned.

If you know despair or can see it in others.

I want to know if you are prepared to live in the world with its harsh need to change you. If you can look back with firm eyes saying this is where I stand.

I want to know if you know how to melt into that fierce heat of living falling toward the center of your longing.

I want to know if you are willing to live, day by day, with the consequence of love and the bitter, unwanted passion of sure defeat.

I have been told, in that fierce embrace, even the gods speak of God.

Our Soul Whispers

Too often we seek to find purpose from ego, but the ego cannot tell us—in fact, does not know—our true purpose. Based on the ego's promptings, we imagine that we would be more effective, more successful, and maybe gain greater admiration from others if we lived by our purpose. These are what the ego wants. Our soul wants something else. Our soul simply wants to be expressed. When we search for our purpose through the lens of our ego, we can't find it, for it doesn't exist there. It exists in a different place in our being, and it speaks to us differently. The soul rarely shouts to us to tell us what it wants. Instead, it whispers. We learn its message by listening to our body—by noticing what resonates with us and what does not. We learn its message by paying attention to our dreams. Our soul lives in our unconscious or subconscious, and rarely does it surface enough to speak its message clearly. When it does surface, we need to be ready to listen.

Our purpose seldom reveals itself all at once. It unfolds in layers. Finding the soul's purpose involves ongoing listening and inquiry. Our soul speaks to us differently in different moments. One time it might appear as a sense or a feeling. The feeling may start as a vague sense of dissatisfaction, or a momentary glimpse of how things could be. Over time the feeling may get more crystalline and take on new forms. It may repeatedly shift shape while its essence remains. To find and live one's purpose requires that we are deeply committed to being in the question, committed to the inquiry process itself. We need to love the question and let the answer unfold, unencumbered by a need for direct communication. Our ego wants pat answers, and if we restrict our inquiry to ego concerns, we narrow our listening and our discovery. Rainer Maria Rilke, often considered the greatest modern lyric poet in the German language, spoke to this eloquently.

> I beg you to have patience with everything
> unresolved in your heart
> and try to love the questions themselves
> as if they were locked rooms
> or books written in a very foreign language.
> Don't search for the answers,
> which could not be given to you now,
> because you would not be
> able to live them.
> And the point is, to live everything.
> Live the questions now.
> Perhaps then, some day far in the future,
> you will gradually, without even noticing it,
> live your way into the answer . . .

I had a dream recently that spoke to the essence of living authentically for me. It came to me as I was imagining the creation of a workshop
related to authenticity. This is often the way the soul works. When you
embrace the question, a dream will emerge to teach you about its message. And sometime in the course of the inquiry, a troubling dream or
nightmare might also emerge as an indicator of the ways that you are
(or have been) moving away from the soul. Nightmares are powerful
messengers of the soul, if only we choose to pay attention.

In my dream, I was teaching a class with my father on something
related to personal growth. In the middle of the class we took a break
as we always did, and for some reason I was compelled to get on my
motorcycle and wander off. In the course of my ride, I forgot completely who I was, or where I was. I knew somewhere deep down that
I had been teaching a class with my father but I didn't know who he
was, where it was, or how to reach him. I continued to drift farther and
farther away, completely lost. Finally, after a couple of hours of riding
aimlessly, I remembered who I was and that I had been teaching a class,
but I had no idea where the class was or how to get back there. I called
my father on my cell phone and he gave me directions to a restaurant
where he and my brother were eating dinner. He was gravely worried
about me, and glad to know that at least I was not injured.

I found my way back to the restaurant and explained my mini-odyssey.
My father assured me he had led the class just fine without me and that
the class would just be glad to know I was okay. As I talked with my father,
my brother was moving and fidgeting in his chair. His movements were
more than distracting; they were violently intolerable. Just as I was about
to ask my brother to stay still, I felt excruciating nausea and subsequently
vomited on the floor. Following that episode I was not only calm but also
completely clear about where I needed to take the class and who I needed
to become. I told my father that he could no longer teach the class with me.

This dream, like most dreams, makes sense in the context of the question I had been sitting with the night before. It tells me that although
the body of work I had been doing was good (worthy of teaching in a
classroom), it was not fully my own, for it was (in the dream) taught in
tandem with my father. In dream interpretation, often the players are

not necessarily to be taken literally. In this case, I think my father represents the part of me that is will-based, conventional, and authoritarian. The ride on a motorcycle suggests a need for freedom, to break away from this part in me and work more directly from my soul. Getting lost was a symbol of being lost in my driven ego and the break that I needed to take in my psyche to find the full expression of who I am. In vomiting, I was purging myself from the last vestiges of living inauthentically. The twitches from my brother are akin to the twitches that we all feel when not fully comfortable in our skin—not fully living from soul. The dream teaches me about my path of fully owning and embracing who I am, and that my work needs to be fully an expression of my soul, untethered to the will-based ego that has been a part of my past.

Our Calling

Few people in Western society have a firm grasp of their life's purpose. We are enthralled with celebrity and conquest and with media images of what constitutes "success." In setting our sights on material goals, we seldom stop and ask ourselves, "Why am I here? What is my true calling?" Without answers to these questions, we drift from job to job and career to career, cobbling together a life we hope is worth living, measuring success in outward terms. Like a peacock displaying its tail, we find gratification in showing the world how successful we are. Look at what I own! Look at what I've done! But we seldom feel satisfied. Returning to Rilke, in Love Poems to God he writes:

Each thing—each stone, blossom, child—is held in place. Only we, in our arrogance, push out beyond what we each belong to for some empty freedom.

To me, this is a poem of the soul—suggesting we each are born with a unique purpose or gift in life that is a natural way of being. It is one of the defining characteristics of humanity that at an early age we lose touch with this nascent experience. The journey of consciousness is the journey back to a place where we once dwelled, inside ourselves.

The older I get, the more I recognize that my early definitions of success now ring hollow. Well into my adult years—especially by my late thirties—something deeper began to stir in me. I was consumed by a yearning, a sense of knowing, that there is more to the measure of one's life. It is this knowledge of living consistent with a deeper purpose that distinguishes and even defines people who feel most fulfilled in life.

In the Christian world, priests and ministers speak of their vocation or "calling," as if called to serve God's purpose. At a more secular level, I once heard it said that a calling is when one's greatest joy meets the world's greatest need. The idea is that we are here on Earth for a purpose, and to live that purpose yields the greatest value for oneself and for the world.

There are a rare few people who know their calling. Even more rare are the ones who know it early in life. I was one of those who knew early on in my heart that I was meant to bring more consciousness into the world. The expression of that purpose has morphed over time, but the experience of clarity of that purpose has not wavered since it appeared to me in my early twenties. However, it was only in my late thirties that I was able to take the next step, from merely knowing my calling to truly embracing it and declaring it fully to the world. Until then, I remained entrapped in society's expectations and my own as I got married, had children, and adopted a variation of the rather conventional male role of "settling down" and being good provider.

Finding one's true purpose can be a difficult challenge, as we have seen. I recently met a young woman on a plane who, in the course of our mutual greetings, asked me what I did for a living. I explained how I am a guide to leaders, helping them embrace and manifest their powerful leadership potential. In due course she confided in me that she was in a major transition in her life, unsure of where she wanted to take her career while sure that the job she was in was not at all satisfying.

This conversation took a very typical course. Whenever I describe myself as a guide to help people live an authentic and fully expressed life, I am often told, "I am in a transition myself," or "I need that, I'm lost," or some variation on that theme. While not conclusive, I would estimate that over 90% of the population feels unsatisfied and lost, feeling little or no connection to their deepest soul's desire.

In describing her efforts to find a more exciting and meaningful career, this woman said she was following the guidance of friends to research alternative careers and see what she liked. But in doing this she was feeling increasingly discouraged and emotionally dead, for none of the possibilities excited or energized her.

Her methods were very typical. It strikes me that most paths to find one's career end with a sense of futility, but not for the reasons that are evident. The primary reason is that we search with our heads and not our hearts, and that our egos are doing the search and not our soul. Our heads are filled with a lifetime of expectations and beliefs about what is right and what is profitable and what is desirable. Our heads are cluttered with the cacophony of messages we've received throughout our life from others who believe they (that is, their egos) know what we should go after. When the ego searches, it searches for definitions of success that might make it feel good, but our soul may have an altogether very different agenda for us.

Part of the reason it is so difficult to find our true path is that we don't know where to turn for guidance. Early on, we turned to our teachers or parents or peers or career experts to help us figure out what to choose as a career or a calling, failing to realize that it is not a process of simply reviewing and checking off available career choices. Our true calling can only be found inside of us.

One very common way we are told to determine our ideal career is to take a test. One of the most popular is the Campbell-Strong test, which is designed to ask you about things you like and value and then tell you which people in which careers seem to match you the most. This test told me that I was best suited to be a policeman or a lawyer. In some ways this was not surprising, for I have both a strong sense of honor and of right and wrong (like many in the police force), and in my younger days I used to love to argue, using logic as a weapon (like law-yers). But when I learned the test results, my soul wasn't buying it. To this day, I acknowledge I might have been a good lawyer—but my soul cringes at the thought. (No offense to lawyers—it's just not who I am.)

Sometimes, we just pick things that we (or others) think we're good at, because we feel we could earn a lot of money or attain prestige. When the drive for money, prestige, or approval becomes the decid-ing factor, our chosen career then becomes truly "soul-killing", even if the conditions under which we work are relatively pleasant and full of perks.

Sometimes we drift from job to job, career to career, hoping that something feels right. If we're lucky, we land on something that might feel remotely satisfying. If we're not, we end up spending half our waking lives in misery—and all our waking lives bereft of our soul's purpose.

I remember hearing a long time ago that by the end of their lives the average person will have had three careers. Many of us bounce around from job to job, opportunity to opportunity, making choices that seem intelligent or expedient at the moment. In each job we embrace the challenge and try to learn how to reach some semblance of mastery so we can earn more money and achieve greater "success"—a poor sub-stitute for true satisfaction. Equally as problematic is the person who hangs on to one career, knowing all in all it is not their true joy.

At the end of our life, we often look back with a deep sense of loss and regret. Almost always the regret is that our career choice took away our life and shriveled our spirit; rarely if ever would we feel that we spent too much time in soul-satisfying activities and not enough in making money.

It is interesting and troubling that we refer to our jobs as "making a living" when in most cases they are merely ways to earn money. Many say "I work to live" or "My work is my life" as if it were a badge of honor. The point is not to value or devalue work as such, but to redefine the purpose of work based on the soul's needs rather than the ego's. Finding a good job cannot be separated from life's primary objective: finding our soul's purpose.

Ambition is the enemy of the soul.

In my younger days, I had sacrificed much in the service of ambition. I had lied in order to get what I wanted. I had put myself in situations for which I was not ready in order to grow and learn, knowing full well I was not the best person for the job. I disguised my inabilities in order to get a job so I could learn. I had blamed others for mistakes knowing full well I had been a player in the creation of the problem, but didn't want to admit it to others, fearing I would not have other opportunities. In so many ways, I had let my ambition drive my choices and in so doing dishonored a deeper truth.

In reflecting on the many moments I have sacrificed my soul, I realize that my ambition and the ambition of all those around me are a huge barrier to the soul's expression. My ambition came to me early in life. Both of my parents were driven in different ways and were also quite brilliant, as were my stepparents. I see now that my own drive and ambition are a direct reflection of my desire for their love. While they loved me, they parceled out their affection in very small doses. This came to be particularly clear to me at the moment I received my doctoral diploma from Harvard University.

As I stepped down from the podium upon receiving my diploma, I saw my mother with her outstretched arms. She had tears in her eyes, hugged me, and whispered in my ear, "I'm very proud of you, Keith." I looked in her eyes at that moment and tears welled up inside of me as I said, "Thank you"; and then we hugged again. At that moment, two simultaneous feelings jolted me. The first was the sense of the deliciousness of hearing that my mother was proud of me. Her love seeped into my pores, like a dry sponge thirsting for water. The second feeling struck me like a lightning bolt: This was the first and only time I remember my mother telling me that she felt proud. What an incredible standard she held for me. It was in achieving the pinnacle of education at perhaps the finest university in the country if not the world that I would finally earn my mother's pride. And if my father was proud of me in my life, I had no awareness of it. In other words, so much of my drive, my ambition to succeed and to excel, was driven by a simple and profound desire to be loved by my parents—or, more to the point, to feel their respect and pride. To be clear, I love both my parents and know they love me. But this was hard for me to feel, especially throughout my early life.

And that is what ambition is for so many of us, perhaps all of us. It is a desire for recognition, to accomplish something and get the goodies that this accomplishment offers, the biggest of which are love, attention and recognition. So many of us parade our fine cars, houses, toys, diplomas, trophies, and honors not because they are valuable in themselves, but in hopes that others are impressed. Ambition is created by the ego for the ego; for the fruits of our labor, when measured in these terms, is a salve for the ego.

Yet ambition does nothing for our soul. As suggested in a poem by the great Sufi mystic Rumi, our soul is here for its own joy, to be honored by oneself. The relationship between wanting recognition and love from others and the ability to simply love oneself is simple. The more I've learned to love, honor, respect myself, the less my ambition. I would say that at this point in my life, at age 54, I feel very good about who I am and who I've become. I love myself, and have little desire or need to mold myself into anything at all.

Not surprising, earning my mother's pride did not stop my ambition at all; the pattern was deeply etched by then and I was driven to want more of it. It was only later, when I no longer felt I needed my mother's pride or my father's recognition and love, that the tide of my powerful ambition was stemmed. It was when I could fill that need in myself that my other-directed ambition finally was dissolved. Moreover, I might add that I have not accomplished many of the things my early adult self set out to do. I am not the consultant to kings and presidents that I aspired to become. But this does not matter, for I am guided by something different, something deeper in me. I simply want to serve and be well used for the gifts that I have and the gift that I am—nothing more.

To live consistent with our purpose requires that we make a choice somewhere in the course of our life to stop following a path of ambition, greed, or being the person we thought we were supposed to be, and instead become the person our deepest heart says we are meant to be. We must stop bowing to the altar of our mind and our ambition and bow instead to the altar of our soul and find its purpose—for its own joy.

An Exercise

How to Find Your Purpose: A Multi-Step Exercise

There are many books in the marketplace that give guidance on how to find your purpose, and it would be folly for me to try to do the subject justice in one chapter. My intention here is not to tell you how, but to offer words that might point you in a useful direction. If you also want the "how", I recommend reading Tim Kelley's book: True Purpose: 12 Strategies for Discovering the Difference You Are Meant to Make.[12]

What I most want to say is that the finding of one's purpose requires that you look with different eyes and you listen with different ears. For the soul does not communicate to you in ordinary ways—it whispers rather than shouts, and it often communicates with symbols and not overt messages. The soul speaks to you through daydreams where you spend time imagining yourself doing things or being in certain contexts. The soul speaks to you through dreams while you sleep. And most importantly, you can know the whispers of your soul by paying attention to your body, for your body knows that which your mind cannot decipher. I am reminded of the wise fox who said to the little prince in the book of that same name by Antoine de Saint-Exupéry, "It is only with the heart that one can see rightly. What is essential is invisible to the eye."[13]

This exercise will be helpful especially if you did not find a sense of purpose in the prior one. Often we have not even allowed ourselves to dream fully, and as a result, nothing in our past reflections gives us guidance. If that is especially the case for you, here is your chance to let loose the boundaries that have kept you from even considering a different future.

To find your purpose, I invite you to begin to allow yourself to have dreams and then to listen to them. Spend a few weeks imagining what you might want to do with your life if unencumbered by money, circumstance, expectation or need. Let the thoughts flow freely. Nothing need be decided at this point. Just let the imagination free itself up. As images and thoughts or feelings emerge, write them down in your journal. If you are so inclined, you might also with to paint pictures depicting the essence of these dreams.

After a few weeks of this, go back and see if you can detect patterns in these words, pictures or images. These patterns may be the soul communicating to you. What message (or messages) are your dreams telling you about your purpose?

I was recently with a group of people that I guide toward living a fully realized life, and one woman spoke about her strong desire to be in theatre as well as to serve others. She is a shining light in many ways, filled with life. Other times, she appears quite angry and reactive. After she shared her desire as well as her sadness that she was stuck in a job that was going nowhere for her, I asked her what kept her from pursuing her dreams. Her answer was simple and direct. "I have this voice in me that says it is impractical and I have to do what is smart—which is to keep my job."

"Where did you learn to listen to such a voice?" I asked, sensing the emotions welling up in her.

"Oh, that's easy. My parents kept telling me I couldn't make it in theatre and that it was impractical. They kept hammering it home to me to the point that I believed them."

"I wonder," I said, "about how much of your anger that you feel in a given moment is really not about the moment, but about a larger feeling of not having honored your deeper desires—and that perhaps you're not living the life you most want to live."

Tears flowed immediately as I spoke these words, which touched a resonant chord. We waited for a bit, honoring the message of those tears, and then she confessed what was now obvious to her—that she was stuck. She asked me, "What do I do?"

As much as I wanted to make it all right and offer the magical potion that would release the tension, I could not, for it is not within me; it is within her. "Sherry, it is simply a choice. No one can make it for you. Nor can I tell you which is best. That is for you to know. I invite you to simply notice the choice you have made many times over, and notice the effect. And then simply continue to make that choice or make a different one. If you choose to follow your deepest calling, know that it too has a consequence."

And with that, she was left with herself to explore, knowing she would be loved no matter what the choice. As we explored, the other members of the group each strongly urged her to choose her soul's desire. Such a feeling is typical, and completely understandable. At the same time, it is misplaced, no matter how sincere and sweet. I offered that the group's desire for her to choose her soul's calling is a desire for themselves, and that rather than their putting pressure on her to make the soul's choice, they might want to see their desire as a reflection of their own inner desire for themselves and to examine and respond to that desire. With that, the exploration deepened for each and for the group as a whole.

As you listen to your past musings, consider the possibility that you've known all along what your soul's calling is but dared not admit it to yourself for it required you to buck the forces of your environment. Consider that along with powerful dreams come powerful fears. The fear has many faces. Sometimes it is fear of the unknown, for there is naturally much uncertainty in leaning into the newly imaged life that is just beginning to form. Sometimes the fear is of loss—often living one's purpose may mean loss of friends, loss of a stable income, or the ridicule of one's family. Sometimes it is fear of being out of control—we know how to navigate and control our old life and seem to need that control to give us comfort.

An Exercise

Continuing our earlier exploration, I invite you to listen to your night dreams for the next few weeks. The best way I know to do this is to go to bed with a question—a desire for your soul to reveal its calling. Ask yourself, in other words, to have dreams that teach you. Those familiar with dream work know that it is hard to remember dreams in the morning. It is fascinating to me how they are so quickly locked back up in our unconscious, possibly because they are messages that our conscious mind does not yet want to hear. Our conscious mind tends to follow the dictates of our environment, and our unconscious mind tends to follow the dictates of our deeper yearning; and to the extent that they are in conflict the conscious mind will want to suppress the messages. To remember and listen to the messages of your dreams requires you to be willing and ready to hear. That is why the process starts with letting go of the shackles. If you are not ready to do so, you soul will not be ready to be heard.

To listen to your dreams, have your journal near your bedside. Tell yourself that you want to hear them and that you will wake yourself up enough to write down its message. Then when you have a dream, wake yourself up and write it down. Don't worry about its meaning. Just write, and then quickly go back to sleep. Keep doing this for as long as you like (preferably 2–4 weeks) and then go back to look at what you've written. By now, if there are seven or so dreams, a pattern will likely be revealed; the pattern may be the whisperings of the soul.

Once you have images of your soul's calling, run them through your body. Imagine yourself being/doing the things your soul suggests and see how it feels. Notice where you feel excited— when your body lights up. Notice where you feel fear. Distinguish between the kind of fear that tells you that you're off track—such as dread, despair, desperation and anguish—and the kind of fear that suggests you're on to something meaningful— such as light anxiety, fear of failure (if it didn't mean anything, then failure would not matter), or fear of loss of control (often associated with the uncertainty of a new venture).

Notice which thoughts or directions cause you to feel deadened in your body and which cause you to come alive. Don't act on these bodily feelings for now; just notice them. Eventually, through the process, it will become clear enough what your purpose is.

Write in your journal what appears to be emerging for you.

Leap Frog

If you find yourself stuck, consider this exercise. We often think in terms of goals. Our images of what is next for us show up often as aspirations just beyond where we are. For example, a truck driver might want to eventually buy his own truck. A ballet dancer might imagine being a teacher of ballet to young children someday. A doctor might think about running his own department at the hospital. We leap in front of ourselves and imagine the next phase.

Imagine yourself at this natural next place. This is often not your soul's desire, but instead a natural extension of where you are. Now leap frog forward and imagine what is next for you, well beyond this place. Let yourself be open and curious as to what wants to emerge. Let your imagination run free, as if there were no constraints. Consider this next phase well beyond your dreams as your soul calling to you, into the possibility of who you might become. Now take the leap once further. Imagine yourself there, having arrived. What feels like "next" even beyond that? Write your thoughts in your journal.

Following Your Soul's Desire

The path of following our soul's calling seems to have some patterns to it. These patterns have been revealed to me only because I've worked with so many people with this aim in mind. The most prevalent pattern is the desire to run away from our purpose or to jump off the path the moment our fears take over. "I can't do it" is often the thought, or "I'm terrified that I'll lose X." Even more frightening is the sense that the person might fail, and to fail in living one's purpose can feel devastating. I have observed over time that the bigger the purpose, the bigger the fear. This equation is inevitable. The bigger the leap from where we are to where our soul's desire calls us, the bigger the potential for failure and the bigger the fear.

An Exercise

As you reflect on the emerging image of your purpose, allow yourself to feel what life might be like were you to live this image fully. What would you be doing? What would you stop doing? How might you be relating to others? What will it feel like? Give yourself room to enter this possibility and feel its rich contours. Write in your journal your thoughts and reflections to these questions.

At the same time that wonderful images, feelings, and thoughts will come to you if you let yourself sink into the experience, what may also come up are fears. These fears are natural artifacts of the ego protecting you. It is the ego trying desperately to hold on to the comfort of sameness in your life, not wanting to risk what you have already. It is natural to have the fears. The key is to hold them in proper relationship and not be governed by them. So for now, simply allow the fears to surface. Be good with the fears. They are part of the path of embracing all that you were meant to be. The fears could be in any of a number of arenas. They could be related to loss of control, loss of relationships, loss of things, and even fear of death. Sometimes it is simply the terror of not knowing, which is another form of fear of loss of control. Write down the fears that come up as you imagine yourself living your purpose. Feel free to use some of the categories below that are simply suggestive to allow for easy reflection.

1. What I fear I might lose that is related to control:

2. What I fear I might lose in my relationships (people who might go away):

3. What I fear I might lose related to my competence (where I imagine or fear I might be less effective):

4. What I fear I might lose in terms of things:

5. Other fears that don't fit neatly into the above categories:

The simple question becomes, which of these will you do—follow your purpose, or follow your fear? The solution is not to try to get rid of fear. Fear is a natural part of the equation. People who are uncomfortable with fear itself inevitably seek comfort over a passionate life. They live life in dull hues. I once was told there was a person who spent years searching for the heart of communication. He never found the key that unlocks its mystery but found something else instead: He learned who the devil is. The devil is the part of us that wants to believe we can live life fully and at the same time be comfortable.

Don't listen to that voice that wants comfort in life. It is an imposter. Wisdom tells us that fear and risk are natural compatriots—they go hand in hand. To the extent that your purpose has risky elements—charting a new territory—fear is along for the ride.

Interestingly, the physical response to fear and exhilaration are one and the same. Remember the feeling on a roller coaster ride—the heart rate quickens, your body gets tingly, anticipation leads to shortness of breath, your breathing gets shallow. Or consider the excitement you felt going on your first date with someone you were excited to be with. The heart pounded, the breath got shallow and if truly smitten, you may have even been tongue-tied.

The same biological responses occur in a dangerous mountain climb or whitewater rafting or facing a dangerous situation. Our body does not know the difference between thrill and fear, between imagined fear and real fear. The key to living an authentic life is to welcome the fear; it is an important friend along the journey. There is enormous wisdom to the dictum, "Feel the fear and do it anyway."

Once you are clear about your purpose, your choice is simple, follow it or let fear take over. That doesn't mean it is an easy choice, it's just a simple one. Don't let your fear quiet the fierce desire of your soul. Heed the words of Rumi in his poem "Quatrains": "Don't go back to sleep."

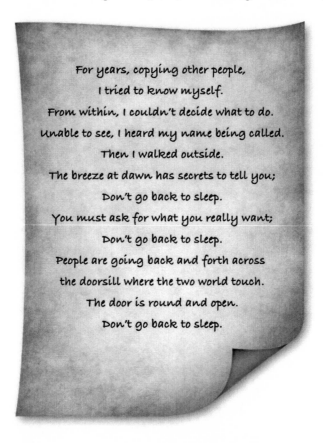

For years, copying other people,
I tried to know myself.
From within, I couldn't decide what to do.
Unable to see, I heard my name being called.
Then I walked outside.
The breeze at dawn has secrets to tell you;
Don't go back to sleep.
You must ask for what you really want;
Don't go back to sleep.
People are going back and forth across
the doorsill where the two world touch.
The door is round and open.
Don't go back to sleep.

Often, along this path of the journey toward purpose, a client will tell me, "I want to live my life's purpose, I just don't know how." It's important here not to confuse "I don't know how" with "I'm afraid to go for it." You can choose and commit to your purpose without knowing. The knowing comes later, once the choice is made, not the other way around. If you wait to choose until you have all your ducks in a row, you are making clarity of movement more important than your soul's desire.

The kind of resolve and determination needed to follow your inner compass is often great. When you hedge your bets by waiting for the path to become completely clear, you are giving in to your desire for comfort and ease and therefore walking the path from a place of fear, seeking safety nets along the way. Don't do it. Don't give in to the desire for certainty, for it will dampen your ability to experience the full range of your purpose. Instead, choose courageously. I have heard it said that commitment is jumping off a cliff and building your wings along the way. Jump into the chasm of your longing, and you and your path will find one another.

An Exercise

I encourage you to consider the following exercise. Once your purpose is clear or clear enough, take some time off in a quiet natural setting somewhere, or find a place that is soothing and soul-inviting for you. Sit with yourself for a while and let your imagination run free. Imagine all the ways you might be expressing your purpose. Listen to your body as you do this, for your body will tell you much about what resonates with your soul and what does not. You body is the barometer of your soul if you allow it to offer its wisdom. When an image resonates, write it down. Allow yourself to feel and imagine the full expression of that image. Then continue to imagine other expressions of that purpose. Keep writing, breathing, listening to what shines brightly and what only comes in dampened hues.

Once complete, take a look at what you've written and see if you can find patterns, patterns that give you clues to the right path. These patterns may form in any of a number of ways. Don't pre-wire the form they take—let your notes and images speak to you. More often than not, more clarity will come to you through the process. Later, you may want to take these images and patterns and form them into a plan. For now let them sing to you their own song.

Ultimately you face a choice. Live your life out of fear, driven by ego, following what society tells you—or live your purpose. It is a choice, pure and simple. When you chose what others tell you, you will face a life of dis-ease and lack of fulfillment. Ultimately, it will affect your body and can become a chronic medical problem. Is it any wonder that in our Western society, where matters of the soul have been chucked away in return for monetary or material gain, our health is deteriorating and so many of us feel disconnected from our own bodies? Is it any wonder that so many of us feel hollow and empty, living a life devoid of meaning? Our compulsive seeking of distractions (like celebrity idolatry, chemical intoxication, and quick thrills) is a way of fleeing the deeper pathos we so often feel and yet are unwilling to own and face.

This does not have to be our life's fate. Since we consciously or unconsciously chose to follow our society's story of what a successful life is, we also have the power within us to choose differently. It is not finding our purpose that is most difficult, although it is certainly challenging for many; the greater difficulty is to heed the soul's call and embark on the great journey back to our deeper self.

CHAPTER SEVEN

LIVING IN INTEGRITY

"To be nobody-but-yourself — in a world which is doing its best night and day, to make you everybody else — means to fight the hardest battle which any human being can fight; and never stop fighting."

– E. E. Cummings

The word "integrity" has many meanings. In common parlance, when we say, "he has no integrity," we often mean "he is not truthful," or "his words don't line up with his deeds." Put simply, we don't trust that person. We will deal with that particular meaning in the next chapter.

I am more interested here in the deeper meaning of integrity, one that often eludes us, partly because we have few ways of understanding it. I am interested in the idea of being integrated—of being whole. In this sense, integrity means being true to all of me—of having my mind, body, spirit and actions all line up. The idea of equating integrity with being whole—with embracing all of who we are—came to us through Jungian psychology. When we have this kind of integrity, this kind of integration, we walk upright, are centered in our psyches and are solid in the world. And when we have this kind of integrity, we honor the deepest truths of others as well.

Most of us grow up in an environment where being integrated is not the focus. Instead, we look upon ourselves and the world through the lens of specialization. We separate out and analyze everything, often much to the detriment of an integrated, whole vision of life. Actually, this way of looking at things started centuries ago.

In the 17th century, for example, René Descartes offered up a vision of cause and effect where, in order to understand a particular phenomenon, one needed to break it down into its elemental parts. Our whole

111

Western society's system of scientific inquiry over recent centuries has been based on this Cartesian model, and we all grew up under the weight of this image.

One of many examples based on this model has been the conventional scientific "wisdom" concerning diet. Recommendations of "experts" almost always centered on a "balanced diet" consisting of three meals a day and containing certain quantifiable nutrients (which were more or less the same, with minor adjustments, for most people). The idea that one could listen to one's body for guidance on such matters, or that eating involved actually paying attention (rather than mechanically scarfing down food), seemed ludicrous. But it turns out that our bodies can tell us a great deal about what we do and should eat.

Western palliative medical research has taught us how to treat symptoms of diseases with medicine and do our best to alleviate the toxic side effects these very same medicines cause. Even to this day, few palliative-minded doctors recognize as legitimate many alternative and more integrative forms of healing that treat the body as a whole system in spite of the overwhelming evidence that holistic approaches are, in the long run, more effective.

In such a world, so often we listen to what we are taught rather than trust what our bodies or our intuition tell us. Having been taught for most of our formative years how to color inside the lines, we have difficulty seeing alternative and perhaps life-enhancing ways of being. While we may want to break free and follow our own muse, we are told instead the virtues of sticking to the tried-and-true in all areas of life. Instead of learning how to formulate our own theories of how things operate, we are taught how to memorize the theories of others. It's as if we are all actors being taught how to portray the characters as written by the playwright interpreted through the lens of the director rather than creating our own plays, born out of the fertile ground of our imagination.

The unique interaction of body, mind, and spirit in each of us forms a signature of sorts that is uniquely our own. Although I was clear at an early age as to my purpose and the path my soul wanted to take, it took me a long time to follow its message wholeheartedly. Early on in life I wanted to do things well, to do things the way they were supposed to be done. Somewhere in the deep recesses of my consciousness I felt that reaching that goal had much to do with learning how others had done it. Sure, I put my own particular spin on what I learned, but I spent a huge amount of effort studying from those that went before me. I was a good student in the classical sense of the term and earned my doctorate from Harvard University at a young age. And I plied my trade for almost 20 years being a good consultant in the way I had been "taught", seeking to emulate the best that I had seen or read about. I also gobbled up books, with four or five books on my bedside at a time, often reading two or three a week.

And while I was a relatively successful consultant and even an author of a book, there seemed to be a mechanical aspect to what I was doing. I had not found my own unique voice until one day in my mid-forties, when a couple of men who had worked with me in the past asked me to lead a group, the goal of which was to help them find their unique gifts and express them in the world. We called it the "gifts group". We invited a number of others to join us, and the members paid me handsomely to guide them in spite of the fact that I said I was not sure I had the expertise to lead the group. But they felt I was a talented facilitator of deep personal growth and as such was amply qualified for what they were asking me to do. I said okay, as long as they gave me room to experiment.

In the wake of my saying "I don't know" and simultaneously giving myself permission to experiment, something magical unfolded. I found myself sourcing ways of working with people far beyond anything I had ever learned or even seen. I was improvising from the get-go, and my ability to create something to meet the moment was astonishing when compared to my past "paint-by-the-numbers" existence.

My intuition was also rapidly growing—or perhaps emerging. I like to think it was always there—I just hadn't trusted it. Instead of trying to figure out what to do when a person presented a deep psychological limitation, I would often ask for silence so I could sense what might serve. In the silence, almost in a flash, I would know what to do. My work with the individuals and the group was quite penetrating, even to the point that all the members were having their own breakthroughs in awareness just as I was breaking from my own mental prison.

Upon reflection, I realize now that for a long time I have had a particular gift for creativity and imagination, but did not see it. For years, fellow consultants would call me and ask for help in how to intervene in a situation or request that I produce a workshop exercise. Often my help was very creative, building something to meet the need of the moment, but I dismissed such a gift as just something I do on the side. And yet consistently my colleagues were amazed at how I could come up with something each time that truly worked with groups. In a similar vein, for years I used by imagination to make up stories to put my children to bed at night, or to create games for them to explore and play. Yet I never saw myself as a creative sort. In fact, I thought of myself as somewhat uptight, overly bounded by convention. My words were well measured and so too my actions.

As my work with the group grew, so did my imagination and my ability to uncover a unique voice in myself. Around five years ago I almost stopped reading other people's books and articles and was deeply compelled to write my own. I have always been a prolific writer, but with a single exception, I was not drawn to write books. I also never saw myself as a good writer—just someone who liked to write. It was as if a dam burst. In the space of four years, I wrote four books, each one pouring out of me easily and freely. During this time, I also began hitting the speaking circuit, seeking to share myself more fully with others.

Interestingly, simultaneous to the creative surge came a growing inability to organize my life. I was rapidly becoming the archetypal artistic type, disorganized and yet filled with boundless creative energy. What has happened in the past six or seven years is that I believe my life has taken the shape that my soul seeks. It is a unique shape all my own, and when I found my voice, my sense of satisfaction also grew in kind.

In the "gifts" group, and ever since, I've become a muse of sorts, helping powerful leaders find the shape that their soul seeks—and with it, new energy, focus, and the ability to achieve extraordinary results. The concept of integrity is no longer a concept, but a real experience, its fruits revealed over and over again.

Enamored with Celebrities

One of the most pervasive symptoms of inauthenticity in our society is the tendency to idolatrize celebrities. In our society it is almost rampant and I see it as a reflection of our shadow. To understand this, we need to understand the psychological nature of projection and the nature of our disowned selves.

The importance of the concept of projection to leading an authentic life cannot be overemphasized. It is simply the tendency to see another through the lens of our own unexamined or unconscious needs and be unaware of it. Let's look at this phenomenon more closely.

We've all had the experience of coming to a snap decision about someone's character without much evidence and then relating to this person as if that conclusion is true. Later, however, we discover that our assumptions were wrong, the result, more often than not, of having projected onto this person some quality that is actually in us. Psychologists define projection as an unconscious or unintentional transfer of our own internal psyche onto an outer object. For example, manager Susan has an employee named George who is consistently late for meetings. She is frustrated by this and reprimands him for his lax approach, which, she says, is becoming a big problem. He, in turn, begrudgingly admits his failing and simultaneously resents the tone she consistently takes with him.

What Susan doesn't see so easily is that she is sloppy about meetings herself, often arriving late or having to reschedule at the last minute. Susan sees in George an aspect of her own personality and rejects it based on her own self-image of reliability, while in complete denial of her tendencies in the same direction. Were she aware of this and compassionate about it, instead of being upset with George, she'd be curious about its source in him and in her and invite them both into an inquiry as to what to do. George, in turn, might welcome the inquiry, knowing there was wisdom to being more reliable.

The problem with projection is not the projection itself, which is unavoidable because it is baked into our human psychology. The problem is that we remain unaware of it—we don't fold our awareness of our judgments toward ourselves and so we remain blind to our own activity.

Our projections have much to teach us about ourselves. Recently I saw an inadvertently funny ad in an Israeli newspaper that drives home the point:

> Female Graduate Student,
>
> studying the Kaballah, Zohar,
>
> exorcism of dymmuks,
>
> seeks mensch.
>
> No weirdos please.

We all project our judgments and our aspirations onto others, and are often unaware that we are doing so. Consider, for example, someone you admire who seems honest and forthright. Whether or not this is so is not the question, for you can never know for certain (especially at first glance); but the fact that you admire honesty suggests that you possess, embrace, or aspire to that same quality.

Projection is an unconscious psychological mechanism. The more that we are unaware of or refuse to acknowledge—or, in effect, "disown"—certain of our own characteristics or tendencies, the more likely we'll project them onto others, convincing ourselves that it is they, not we, who embody this particular characteristic. In the case of a positive projection, we will cast an individual in glowing terms, failing to recognize it as our own characteristic or aspiration. In the case of a negative projection, we harbor harsh judgments about the other, failing to recognize they embody a characteristic in ourselves that we have not owned as ours.

In Jungian terms, that which is disowned (whether a positive or a negative quality) is our shadow—the part of us that we cannot yet see. By learning to identify when projection is occurring—when qualities of yourself may be peeking out from behind your own shadow—and by owning or embracing these qualities, you begin to sow the seeds of your own metamorphosis into the authentic expression of the person you were meant to be.

If you idolize people who are courageous, for example, consider for a moment that they might be reflecting your own courageous tendencies or potential. Own it and thus embody it more fully! If you find yourself judging people who are rebellious, consider the possibility that there is a strong independent person inside you aching to get out. Perhaps it won't emerge in the form of rebellion but as a creative urge for self-expression. Such is the process of inner mastery—becoming more fully aware of that which is hard to see.

An Exercise

In your journal, write down the names of five people you admire. They can be historical characters, people you know personally, friends, family members. Write down their names in a column on the left of your journal and next to each name, write down the qualities or characteristics you admire about that person. Feel free to use the model below and any other means of describing your positive experiences of that person.

Now consider that each of the qualities you wrote about is a reflection of you. You could not possibly admire these people for these qualities or virtues unless they were values resident in you. By seeing these characteristics in others, you are in effect projecting your values onto them. Whether or not you believe they are your values does not matter. They must be, for if they were not, you would not have admired these things in others.

We don't necessarily know yet whether these are your deepest held values, but we know they are likely to be among your important values. Just let these qualities you wrote down sit there for a while; no actions need be taken.

The process of finding one's own shape and discovering one's deepest desires is often not easy, for the messages are not always clear and distinct. It is like a mystery to be solved, the clues of which are not always apparent. I am reminded of Plato's parable of the cave. Plato offered that life is a mystery and that we can never know fully what is true. All we can see are the shadows. Borrowing loosely from Plato's allegory of the cave, picture a group of people in a dark cave. In the center of the cave is a fire. The people are moving about, but all you can see are the shadows on the wall, somewhat distorted and ever moving. You cannot know what is truly going on by seeing the shadows; all you can do is make some guesses. Such is the nature of life and especially of the exploration of one's inner soul. Projections are some of the clues—the shadows on the wall. Our job is to pay attention to our own projections and be curious as to what they teach us about ourselves. This is the essence of self-mastery—the ability to know oneself fully.

This movement toward inner mastery marks the most important step in the quest to discover your own essence—the set of behaviors, beliefs, and values that are distinctively yours. It is only when you claim yourself that you start to take control of your destiny and become the person you were meant to be. This is the full sense of what I mean by integrity, and when you find and live from that place of integrity you finally arrive at home in yourself. To reach this place requires a passionate desire to plumb the depths—to find, express, and live from the calling of your soul. It means that you must face your inner demons— your inner critic, your doubts, and your fears—for nothing less will get you there. There are no short cuts, no magic pills, no sprinkles of fairy dust for achieving the inner knowing from which self-mastery emanates. And, paradoxically and equally important, you can't get there if the desire comes from ego. It's not about adding a notch to the career holster but about surrendering to all that you are in service to something greater.

An Exercise

I invite you to schedule an hour or two in a place where you will feel completely unencumbered by distraction—where you will be able to let your fertile mind run free. In a space in your journal, write down 8–12 events in your life where you felt the greatest sense of ease, satisfaction, fulfillment and joy. Using the model below, write these moments in the space above the line, and write the date or time period in which they occurred in the space below the line. (No need to be precise on dates.)

I recommend that you search for moments that are of special significance to you even if they may not seem special to an outside observer. Certain types of events—an extraordinary trip or pilgrimage to a special place, a public acknowledgment or award, giving birth—evoke happiness universally, but this exercise will be more effective if instead you look for moments that may seem externally ordinary but matter a lot to you.

Birth   **Now**

Now, in the space below each moment or event, briefly describe what meaning it had for you. Ask and answer the question: What is it about this experience that causes me to choose it as a satisfying moment or event? Put differently, what meaning did that event have for you?

Now comes the hard part. Look at all you've written so far in the exercise about people you admired and the events you described and see if you can begin to connect the dots. These are pieces of information, and like shadows on the cave walls, offer clues, not pat answers. What patterns do you see, and what do those patterns begin to tell you about the shape of your soul? Allow yourself to see these events and the people you admire not so much for themselves, but as messages from your unconscious that are seeking to be revealed. What is your soul telling you about itself?

On another page in our journal, on the left hand side, write down your values or principles as they become clear. It usually works best if you have 4 to 7 of these, in order that each can be easily remembered. Next to each value, on the right hand side of the page, write down what that value means to you. For example, to some, the value of honesty means to speak one's truth to others; to others self-honesty may be primary. To some excellence means striving to perfection; to others it means being all you can be, which may not involve any image of perfection. What is most important here is that you define it for yourself.

Knowing One's Values Is Not Enough

Have you ever wondered why so many people can have strong religious convictions and also believe in the justness of war? How can each party to a war believe God is on their side and not on the other?

War is not the only theatre in which unconscious duplicity is played out. To cite a less dramatic but very common example, have you ever wondered how someone can say one thing while intending to do another? For example, many of us claim to value excellence, but then accept something substandard. The incongruity is rampant and obvious to many people, yet it is widely accepted and goes unquestioned. We live in a world where integrity appears to have eroded.

There is an old Italian saying that gets to the heart of the issue: Tra il dire e il fare, ce in mezzo il mare. It means: there is an ocean between the saying and the doing. This is particularly true when it comes to values. Identifying one's values is easy. Living consistent with them—being in integrity—is the hard part. This kind of integrity separates those who feel at ease in their body and in their lives from those who don't. For some it takes clarity to live in integrity. Once they are clear, it is easy to following their inner guidance. For others it takes huge courage.

I often wonder about the fact that so many of us espouse a set of values with great pride and then violate the very same values in day-to-day life. What would cause us to do so?

As is often the case, it comes back to the ego. The problem is not that we don't have values. The problem is that there are competing forces inside us. In addition to our values, we have ambition, pride, desire, lust, fear, and basic survival needs. Each of these may come to the fore at any moment and cause us to compromise those principles we hold near and dear.

We have all lied, cheated, bent the truth, betrayed confidences and friendships, and placed self-interested pragmatism above the welfare of others—even those we most love. In the act, we have felt the powerful dilemma of knowing we were doing something that violated a deep principle and doing it anyway. Sometimes it's a difficult choice; at other times we try to bypass the difficulty by being in denial or shutting down our feelings. We may rationalize that our choice to violate our principles was the only option; yet, time and time again, it is the people who make the principled choice who end up feeling good about themselves and maintaining or gaining the respect of others.

I had a recent experience that is difficult for me to publicly admit, which brought home for me the challenge I've described. For the first time, I became a spammer. I bought a list that was collected precisely for the purpose of sending a message to people who had not opted in. I justified the action by saying to myself that everyone does it and I need to do it too in order to be as successful as I can be. In other words, I did this in order to help myself. At a deeper level it was because I did not trust the more natural and legal ways in which messages get out into the world. Even more deeply, I was not trusting that the universe provides. For the first time in years, I knowingly violated my principles.

For weeks I struggled with the decision. Am I being fair to others and to myself? In the end I decided to go for it, knowing full well that it was not done with integrity. I think at some level I felt like I deserved to bend the rules a bit and take the advantage of this possibility as so many others had done. Yes, when we all cheat the system, the integrity of the system suffers. In spite of that, I decided for once to override my own principles.

I regretted the decision from almost the moment I made it. And then I got caught. Someone complained and my Internet provider intervened and levied a fine. I paid it knowing that what I was doing was penance of sorts, taking my punishment for a crime that I committed willingly and knowingly.

At some deep place in me, I felt relieved having paid the penalty. I had done damage and responsibly paid the price. In so doing, I felt some degree of temporary relief.

But the sense of shame did not go away, because paying a penalty did not change the facts of the situation. Here I was, professing to others the importance of integrity—coming across as one who had mastered that area of life and was teaching others to do the same—when I had just violated my own in a big way. I felt a strong sense of shame not just for doing what I did, but for being an imposter—one who professes one thing but does not act consistent with the very thing he professes.

In my case, the only true relief will come—in fact, already has come in a large degree—from acknowledging completely how I orchestrated my own violation, and coming to peace with the choice I made and the awareness that I have more learning to do to trust the universe. It does not matter to me if you say this is a small thing or not. For me the dynamic of facing myself and how I came to the choice is the only salve. One must learn through unremitting self-honesty—without judgment but without turning from the truth of one's situation.

I would not have gone to such length if this were simply my own story. In fact, this is a universal human story. It is the same pattern that afflicts us all—the battle between our soul and our ego. You've seen this same battle depicted in somewhat comic form in so many movies, when the devil and an angel are perched on each shoulder, speaking in each ear. Both voices are there. If we listen to our ego, represented by the devil, we may gain something in the short run, but this pales in comparison with what is sacrificed.

The biggest thing that is lost is that by choosing to violate our integrity we are violating the sense that we are all connected. We are reaffirming our separateness in the world (or the illusion of separateness), and in so doing, we end up feeling less connected, less able to take in the life-energy that surrounds and supports us. That is a far bigger loss than any punishment levied on us—either by ourselves or by society.

Instead, what we unconsciously do is play out a process that we have assimilated from our Judeo-Christian culture. (It may in fact be a perversion of the truths behind these religions, but nevertheless it is what has been handed down to us.) This process, in many ways, keeps us from the deeper awareness of ourselves that is available to us. The pattern is this: We sin, cheat, lie, or violate another. We get punished for it. We do penance of some form and feel remorse. We are then forgiven. As long as we know this game and feel accepted back into the tribe of our friends, family, and church after having done penance, we feel fine, because we know we get to sin again and again and get absolved again and again. The cycle is SIN, FORGIVENESS, and SIN. Rinse and repeat.

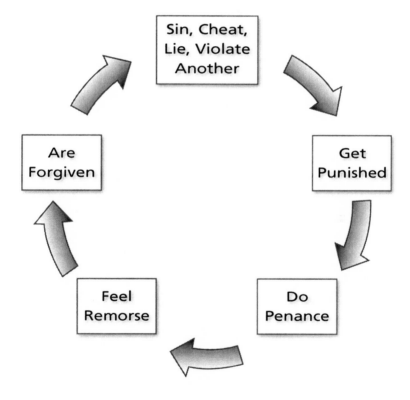

Figure 7–1: The Sin-Forgiveness Cycle

This is not to downgrade the importance of forgiveness in our lives. Forgiveness is necessary and is extraordinarily healing. But the forgiveness rituals we enact are nowhere near enough. The cost of the violation of our values is far greater than we imagine, for what is lost is remembering that we are connected. Indeed, in its truest sense one cannot even be forgiven without a restoration of this sense of connectedness. Forgiveness without connectedness is impotent. And connectedness— to the world, and to our own soul—is necessary before we can recognize and reclaim our own divinity. Institutions and hand-me-down rituals cannot do this for us.

The good news is that, in practical terms, all we need to do to reclaim our divinity is to respect the consequences of the choice we made and then recommit to remembering that we are all connected. In so doing, something can be claimed or reclaimed in the process.

When you think of people who act with integrity, what feelings come to mind in relationship to that person? For most of us the feelings would likely be admiration, respect, and trust. You may also feel a sense of awe. How is it, you may ask, that they live a life that seems so conscious, so bountiful, so pure? Chances are they don't. Chances are however, they have demonstrated valor under pressure or done something that you deeply respect—even if you say to yourself, "I could never do that." Well, you can! You are no different than they are, except that perhaps you are so identified with your own inner violations that you feel small. It is this sense of smallness that gives you a sense of awe of their bigness. I felt small when I did what I did with the spamming and it is because I was playing a small game. By owning up and choosing to never do it again or violate my integrity in any way, have the chance to truly welcome a bigger game in the future.

An Exercise

Take your list of principles and do an inventory of your life. In this inventory, you are invited to identify all the ways in which you live consistent with each principle and all the ways in which you don't. First take each principle (or value) and give yourself a number on a scale of 1 to10, where 10 is that you live that value 100% (to the best of your knowledge), and 1 means not at all.

Then below each value or principle, list the positives and negatives in your journal. List on the left hand side of the page the ways you behave consistent with each value, and the right hand side the ways your behavior is inconsistent with the value. Be sure to be brutally and lovingly honest with yourself. If you like, you might consider asking people close to you and whom you trust to rate you in these areas as well.

From the list of 5 to 7 items, consider choosing 3 to 5 that you want to work on and develop. Now create a practice that will raise your experience of yourself to a high level (9 or 10). Make a commitment with yourself to live impeccably by this value for one month. If that feels daunting, try it just for one week and see what your experience of yourself is like during and after that week.

A Subsequent Exercise

As a reminder to yourself, create a card that you can fit in your wallet that lists the values or principles you seek to live more fully by. Make the principles as clear and concise as you can.

When I did this exercise 23 years ago, the values I sought to live by more consistently were:

- Spontaneity
- Love
- Brutal Honesty
- Acting Purposefully

At the end of each day, do an inventory of your life and write down in a journal times you behaved consistent with the principle and times you behaved inconsistent with it. Be honest with yourself.

For each moment you notice you were inconsistent, think or feel into what was going on for you. What were you not able to face? What were you protecting? What did you fear? What limiting beliefs did you have? Be honest with yourself and do your best not to judge.

Then, instead of being hard on yourself, honor the choice you made and see if you can feel the consequences. Feel the effect in terms of safety and also in terms of what you lost. Again, don't be judgmental about it. Just do your best to honestly describe these consequences.

Then after you sense your internal obstacles to acting on the basis of your principle, imagine what it would be like to have lived your principle fully in that moment. Allow for a clear image to emerge in which you see yourself as acting in alignment with your principle. How does living in integrity feel? Keep doing this process for weeks, months, and even years. You will see noticeable effects over time.

After having done this exercise over 20 years ago, the effect was profound. I put the principles listed above on a card and each day, at the end of the day for about 10 minutes, I inventoried the day and reflected on moments that were consistent and inconsistent with each principle. When inconsistent, I noted in a journal what was going on inside of me—my fears, limiting beliefs, assumptions—and then I imagined how I could have handled the moment to be completely consistent with the principle. Little by little over the months, something magical occurred. I found fewer and fewer inconsistencies to the point where two years later, I let go of the card. I didn't need it any longer. To this day, 23 years later, I remember the principles and feel that I am much more able to live them easily, as they have become integrated in me so fully.

Of course, I have more to learn, as indicated by my choice to spam others. The choice stands out not only because it was a violation, but because that kind of violation has become rare for me. And for that, I celebrate the learning I have done as a result of this process.

CHAPTER EIGHT

SPEAKING YOUR TRUTH

*"Security is mostly a superstition. It does not exist in nature,
nor do the children of men as a whole experience it.
Avoiding danger is no safer in the long run than outright exposure.
Life is either a daring adventure, or nothing."*

– Helen Keller

"Can I be perfectly frank with you?" were the words that tumbled out of my colleague's mouth. I have heard those words many times in a variety of forms in my life, and so have all of us. They are subtle reminders that there are times we are not frank. The same thing is true of the phrase, "well, to be honest..." By saying this, we are implying that there are times that we're not.

Our language reflects the deeply ingrained cultural assumption that full frankness and honesty are the exception. We bend the truth to meet our needs in so many ways—to protect ourselves, to be sure we're not hurt, to avoid full disclosure of something unpleasant, to protect the other person from being hurt (and in so doing, to protect ourselves from the discomfort of their viewing us as the source of their pain).

While all of our efforts to bend the truth may sometimes seem like an intelligent choice in a dog-eat-dog world, and may indeed provide some immediate advantages, this habit has a much larger negative consequence worthy of attention. Any time we bend the truth to "protect" others, or ourselves, we keep ourselves small, unable to live in the truth of life. It is like buying time, with steep interest. Eventually we will have to face the truth and have others face our truth—or be "found out" as being untrustworthy (either all at once or through gradual attrition of relationships). Until then, we pile untruth upon untruth.

Like an addiction, with each untruth it gets harder to break the pattern and more "convenient" to continue with the pattern. Progressively, we reduce our ability to deal with whatever is present in the moment.

Whenever we bend the truth to "protect" others, it keeps the other person small as well. It is an act born out of our belief that they cannot handle the truth or that we cannot handle a person's reaction to our communication of the truth. In the guise of protecting them we are viewing them as emotionally and intellectually incapable of hearing our truth (and thereby partaking of an honest relationship). Also, we are most likely not believing we can handle their reactions—in other words, we don't trust our own emotional and intellectual capacity for honesty.

Killed by Kindness

We live in a world where being nice is valued. And indeed being nice can have real value—but when is being "nice" not so nice? One may appear kind, even attempt to be truly kind, but being kind may be a protection against acknowledging or telling the truth—a way to "keep the peace" to avoid having to be truthful. Or, being nice may even be viewed as an acceptable way to hide contempt or indifference. When someone says something nice to another and then, after that person leaves, states their true (and often very judgmental) feelings to themselves or another, I don't see that as nice at all, but as destructive. When I see someone trying to act gracious or hyper-functional when in fact that person is feeling depleted, the result of denying one's own needs can be detrimental to that person and to others. In such a case, face-saving pride or misplaced loyalty may be getting in the way of honesty. When I see someone who is not feeling kind, but says something kind motivated by their sense of propriety, I don't see that as nice or helpful; I see that as dishonoring the truth. In the service of being nice, we do an injustice to much that I believe is sacred in the world.

Niceness is too often the clothing that we wear in the world to avoid being seen or to avoid the deeper truth. It is an act that keeps us from the truth of who we are and how we feel. Often we can easily sense a person being disingenuous in their expression of niceness. We can feel the mistrust of that person in our bodies—and yet, under the same guise, we don't call it out, for nice people in our nice culture don't challenge others when they appear to not be genuine. We just experience them as faking it, and feel our bodies pulling away or contracting—and yet we don't speak our truth directly to the person, thus perpetuating the deceit. Instead, we say to someone else, "I just don't trust that person," thus keeping our true feelings and our true self unavailable to the target of our feelings.

It is difficult to feel safe when in the presence of someone who puts on airs of graciousness while trashing that person or group in private. And it is also hard to trust someone whose true opinions and self-expression are stifled by the filter of niceness or civility. What I do love, though, is genuine kindness and graciousness when it is genuinely expressed. When a person's expression and inner experience are aligned, and what emanates from their body, their energy, their words, and their deeds is true kindness, I am deeply moved and called to be kind in return. In the wake of genuinely gracious and kind people, I am moved to wonder why I'm not more kind to others in my life. I am often kind in many ways, and I'm also aware that I can sometimes be selfish and self-serving and be unaware of it to the point that it rankles others at times. I have much to learn from people who are genuinely kind and giving, for they reflect back to me what I am, what I am capable of, and what I have more to learn about in life.

An Exercise

Before reading further, I'd like you to do a brief exercise. Consider all the feelings, all the thoughts, all the judgments, both positive and negative, that have been left unexpressed in your life. In your journal, write down all the things you feel about people in your life that you have not told them. On the left hand column of your journal, write the name of a person who is close to you. In the middle column, write the things that you have not said, for whatever reason. On the right hand column, write the reasons you have for not saying them. These reasons will likely be what you were (or are) protecting, what you were afraid might happen, what you believed would be the consequence, or the like.

After doing this, look back on what you wrote and see if you can detect any meaningful patterns. What are you protecting? What fears are driving you? Is there a thread that seems to connecting your responses?

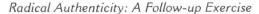

An Exercise

Radical Authenticity: A Follow-up Exercise

Consider for a moment the possibility of living every moment completely in the truth of what is, and with the ability to gently express that truth no matter what. Consider what might have to shift in you to live this way. In what situations would you be most challenged to do so? What is the price you pay for holding back? What is the price others pay?

There is a notion that has been with me for a long time—that of expressing what is true with "no withholds"—in other words, to never withhold the truth from any other human being, no matter what. It is a radical notion that requires courage and deftness. Now I am not talking about telling everyone what you think and feel at all times no matter what. To do so would be folly, for we all have many thoughts and feelings that are immaterial or simply destructive. I am talking about sharing whatever is meaningfully true for you and not withholding—and this means not withholding the good as well as the bad. This would apply to all thoughts and feelings you have about another or about a situation that is meaningful to you and worthy of being communicated. To have no withholds would be to communicate those fully, risking the consequence of others not liking what you say or being upset with the truth of it.

Too often people withhold the truth out of fear of hurting others and in the name of protecting others from their own truth. They see this as caring (and perhaps it is), but it exacts a heavy price. To withhold one's own truth out of fear or concern for another's reaction holds the other person as small, as unable to handle what is true. By taking responsibility for and protecting them from their own reactions, we treat them as less than. Moreover, we treat our own truths as unimportant. Neither appears desirable in my view. Most people fear doing so because they know they have many judgments of others and that it would be unkind to express them. And I would agree if these judgments were simply spewed out in an outburst of anger or frustration. But what if we were inquisitive about our judgments and made a choice to express them in a way that owned them completely as ours. For example, you might say, "I'm noticing I have a judgment about what you are doing. I fear telling you because I don't want to push you away. At the same time, I can tell it is there for me. I believe the fact that I have a judgment is my issue and my problem. I want you to know because I'm struggling with it and it is in the way of me being close or accepting of what you are doing. In other words, I'm struggling with myself."

Now go back to your exercise above and see what you might learn about yourself and what you are protecting, who you are protecting, and where you are struggling to find a way of expressing yourself. If you are like most people, you are withholding your truth as a way of protecting others and ultimately to protect yourself. Consider this and write the ways you are protecting others and yourself. There may be other factors in your withholding, but see if you can dig deeper and find the protectors in you at play.

People who live life fully and authentically care about their own truth and also that of others. They find ways to express the truth in a way that others can hear it, and then hold others compassionately as they face themselves in response. In so doing, they are honoring both ends of the communication—giving and receiving—and the need to be sure the message is heard in the spirit in which it was intended.

I recently witnessed a beautiful exchange in a men's circle that illustrates the point. This is a men's group that I participate in that meets once a month to deepen our relationship to ourselves and to life as a whole. I have found, by the way, that in my journey toward inner freedom, support from other members of the community has been crucial. This has been the function of my men's group for me. None of us is alone and to the extent that we are so bombarded by messages that keep us from experiencing and expressing our soul and divinity, being surrounded by others who support us in being ourselves is a crucial countervailing process. Now, back to the story.

In our circle, one man (we'll call him Jeff) confronted another (we'll call him Bill) and said, "I've been feeling troubled about our relationship and I want to talk about it."

"Okay," replied Bill with a sense of tentativeness that suggested he was unsure whether he really wanted to hear it.

Jeff continued. "I want you to know that I'm sharing this with you not because I am convinced of what I feel but because I want to get closer to you and I find myself having difficulty."

"So talk to me."

"I just don't trust you," said Jeff with boldness and conviction. "I know it has something to do with me, and perhaps with you. I want to explore this with you to see what we might learn."

"Funny," replied Bill, "I don't trust you either." And so began an extraordinary exploration of the source of the mistrust and the ultimate realization that each individual in such a dynamic carries some quality that is needed by the other and that is disowned. Bill is quite outspoken, inclined toward raw expression, but at the same time afflicted with a tendency to trample on others. He lives life with great aliveness. Jeff is quite reflective, inclined toward being gentle. He rarely if ever tramples on others, but instead has difficulty finding his own truth. Jeff lives with gentleness and his life force is relatively subdued. When Jeff and Bill began to share these feelings and their deep desire to get to the truths beyond them, they were able to be compassionate with themselves and each other, and to see the other as an aspect of their disowned selves. By remaining in and fully exploring that space, they found a deep level of love and honoring.

While it may be hard for another to hear the judgment or for you to give it, it may also be freeing for you and the other to fully inspect that which had been tying up so much energy and preventing an authentic relationship. The result is often improved self-respect, a newfound respect for the other, and even a new sense of intimacy between you.

Not only do we withhold our anger, frustrations, and judgments with others, but we also withhold our enthusiasm or tender feelings, often for fear the other person cannot handle it or might judge these feelings as strange or inappropriate. Such withholds are self-protective in nature as well and keep ourselves from expressing our greatest pleasure.

All of our feelings, judgments, and views are ours and ours alone; others may or may not have the same judgments about that person or thing, and the person or group being judged should not feel implicated. If this is so, and if a negative judgment is just our own ego-protective mechanism at play, why would we share it with another?

That question may be answered in any of the three following ways: (1) If you see it clearly as your own issue, driven by your fears and ego needs, then it belongs in the arena of self-exploration and does not need to be shared at all. Therefore it is not a "withhold" to keep it to yourself. (2) If it is getting in the way of you and another person being completely free and open with each other because you have not managed your own issue, then sharing would be relevant—not as a way to dump your feelings onto them, but rather as a way of sharing something you "own." If you are able to embrace your judgments and anger and treat them for the learning and deepening they offer, then sharing your discoveries with another can be appropriately shared in a caring context. (3) Finally, to the extent that the other person may want to learn from your feedback and observations, including your discomfort about things they might be doing (and perhaps be unaware of), then such sharing can be an act of deep kindness and helpfulness.

A System for Understanding Ourselves

One of the most powerful and useful systems for understanding oneself is a system called Voice Dialogue, developed by Hal and Sidra Stone. Their premise is that we are made up of many selves and that growth, development, and psycho-emotional maturity depend on our ability to both understand those selves and to have mastery over them. Such a premise is not new. It has been explored in many different psychospiritual theories and systems of practice, including Psychosynthesis, the work of G.I. Gurdjieff, and Jungian psychology, to name a few. What is rather new in the Stones' system is the unique form of practice they have developed, the essence of which is actually having a dialogue with our different parts.

By actively asking questions of those parts or selves and understanding where they come from, their function in one's own inner cosmology, and how they get triggered, one can gain enormous insights. The more you dialogue, the more you understand yourself. The more you understand yourself, the more you are able to make conscious choices.

Before I make further comments on the Voice Dialogue System, I'd like to examine the roles these parts may play in my life and yours. I have found that to understand who we truly are at the deepest levels requires that we understood the different parts of ourselves—our different "voices," if you will.

One part that I find is often present in me is the part that negotiates. That part of me looks at the world in terms of fairness and reciprocity. That part wants to be sure I don't lose out, or that others don't gain more than I do. It is the part that also wants to be sure I don't gain more than others. For example, I recently had a difficult conversation with my ex-wife in which she asked me to take my daughter for a period of time in exchange for another time. For various reasons I felt resistant to her proposal, as if my needs did not receive equal weight, and the part of me that seeks "fairness" and reciprocity was triggered. Rather than simply owning these feelings, I became focused on the details of our "negotiations" based on my sense of what was fair. I find that I get activated in this way with my ex, and at times I appear to her as stingy. Her response is that I'm "nickeling and diming" her, and indeed, that is exactly what this "negotiator" in myself is doing. Perhaps needless to say, she did not enjoy this interaction. But the "negotiator" in me didn't care; all it wanted was its fair due.

There is another part of me that is pure love—that gives freely without needing anything in return. This part of me understands that we are all connected and that it does not matter if there is imbalance—for as I give, so too do I naturally receive, directly or indirectly. This part of me appreciates the law of karma, knows that doing good is sufficient, and doesn't calculate or care about the return. This part of me freely offers my time and my goodwill, graciously and fully, and derives pure pleasure in the act of giving in itself. It is a part that (in the understanding we have already gained in this book) emanates from my soul and is informed by my sense of divinity.

In contrast, the ego-activated parts of me, such as were activated in my exchange with my ex-wife, are identified with "my" (or the ego's) survival. One of these voices is my ambitious and calculating side. This side has a particular definition of success, and that definition is focused on achieving results in this world for this separate human being. This part believes in my talents and believes that if I go for it, I can achieve just about anything I set my mind to. This part measures success in terms of monetary gain, possessions, status and prestige. It doesn't matter to this part whether others get theirs or not, as long as I get what I deserve and what I earn. This part plays to win and doesn't care if others lose. Giving is done in a calculated way, with expectation of returns. This part of me thinks about whether giving will further my emotional bank account. Will I get opportunities as a result of giving? Will I get noticed? Will I get appreciated, and will doors open to me as a result?

To the extent that I am in a world where my giving comes in the form of my skills and talents in helping others, such a part can be quite manipulative, and so subtle about its manipulation that it can go undetected by me. If I give freely and my motivation appears pure, this giving and this perceived motivation could also enhance my stature in the community and increase the degree to which people will want my services. After all, they will trust me more. The ambitious part of me knows that and sees that I can easily appear to give freely when in fact it is a subtle exchange designed to get something in return. Thus, the part of me that is pure love may have the purest motivations, while my ego-driven, ambitious and calculating side may want to use these pure motivations to its advantage. If we give in to this side—to the ego—even motivations that start out pure can be (and often are) contaminated. We all play many of these games, and are often completely unaware of it.

Ambition and opportunity are not the only reasons we try to control others. Insecurity is another reason. We try to control others as well as our environment in order to feel safe. Like my ambitious side, my insecure side is also involved in a survival game—where the ego is presumed to be the self that survives.

There is yet another role we play—another voice inside of us—involved in survival. That is our inner critic, designed to be sure we don't make mistakes. When we do, it lets us know. In Freudian terms, it is my superego. In the language and understanding of this book, the superego is also very much a part of the ego. It is involved in the same game of survival of the separate self (identified with the ego).

These are but a few of the many selves or voices that live in me and that live in you (to varying degrees with each individual). Myths and legends abound that contain universal archetypes depicting these qualities or roles, as Jung and his successors have pointed out so well.

What is my truth?

In the "voice dialogue" system of understanding, then, we are made up of many voices or truths, each having its own way of seeing and thinking. The question is: which truth or truths do I share with others? Too often people confuse the idea of authenticity with communicating anything and everything. Such confusion can easily cause damage and can lead to all the problems we see around us—from defamation to polarized gridlock to violence, even war. Often we may feel judgment, resentment, and violent anger. When we express this (partial and misleading) truth, unable to see the deeper forces that give rise to these feelings, we often can cause damage under the guise of truth, honesty, and integrity. Let's explore an example of what I mean.

Jack is in a crucial role in his company, working on a product that could propel the company to the next level. Jack went home after a big argument with his boss, claiming he was sick. He then sent an email blast to his boss saying, in effect, "I can't stand working with you. I'm sick and tired of being told I'm a problem when I've been working my ass off. The pressure's killing me and you're to blame. You're a controlling bastard."

Jack's boss, Art, talked with the CEO and together they discussed whether to terminate Jack on the spot, sensing that if they didn't, Jack, who is clearly disgruntled and out of control, would potentially steal the company's blueprints that he had developed. They called the head of the Legal Department who confirmed that the company was protected if they decided to fire Jack for insubordination.

Armed with backup, Art's plan was to confront Jack, demand an immediate apology, and if one was not forthcoming, fire Jack on the spot. To Art's credit, prior to enacting his plan, he talked with the head of HR who suggested that Jack's behavior wasn't insubordination at all, but a sign of distress. After much back and forth, the head of HR convinced Art that a heavy-handed approach would likely not only cause Jack to bolt completely, but also increase the likelihood he would feel justified in his accusations. Moreover, if feeling aggrieved, he might indeed try to hurt the company in retaliation.

In exploring this with the head of HR, Art could see that his first reaction, one of anger and fear, was driven by his need to protect himself and to protect the company, and that it was unwise to act from this place in himself. While it would have been "truthful" to express his anger toward Jack, it was a temporary anger born out of his own fear, and thus it would not have served in any way. Instead, Art chose to get off his high horse and find the place inside him that was genuinely compassionate—open to the possibility that Jack was sending a distress signal—and the way to respond to such a signal is with an open heart. In other words, Art shifted to a different place in him and chose to speak from that place. He met with Jack and began the meeting with an apology to Jack for being the kind of boss that would cause Jack so much upset.

Jack immediately apologized for his email tirade, acknowledging it was childish and not a reflection of the kind of person he wanted to be. Art acknowledged that the email stung and that he was not okay with that kind of communication, but that he understood why Jack felt the need to write it. Jack heard the feedback openly and considered for a bit why he would communicate in a way that violated his own set of standards for communication. Together they discussed openly the pressure they were both feeling. Art admitted his heavy-handedness, which devolved into over-controlling behavior—certainly not how he wanted to be. Jack, in turn, admitted that he tends to act like John Wayne and not ask for the help he clearly needs to finish the project. Together, they figured out a way of working more effectively together.

On the surface, each party had felt aggrieved by the other, and anger and resentment showed up. You could argue that by blasting each other, they would each be speaking their truth and acting with integrity. I would suggest, however, that a deeper truth had been missing, and until that deeper truth is spoken, they are not fully in integrity. They would be expressing the truth of their surface emotions and not their deeper, hard-to-find, more vulnerable emotions. And that is the problem. When we tell our (partial) truths in the name of authenticity and truth, we create big messes. Anger causes defensiveness and invites blame, while the deeper truths of hurt, fear, anxiety and shame—and the deeper desire for mutual healing—are left unexamined and unexpressed.

Illuminating the Shadow through Voice Dialogue

Voice Dialogue is perhaps the most effective practice I have learned for seeing my whole self more fully and clearly and owning the parts that were heretofore in my shadow. Carl Jung spoke about the shadow not in the way we typically understand it, but in a way that is far more subtle and powerful. When most of us think of a person's shadow, we think of their dark side—parts of themselves that we deem to be negative. To Jung, in contrast, the shadow consists of those parts that we cannot see, for they are in our unconscious. In other words, our shadow is the disowned part of ourselves. Jung believed that the path of enlightenment and fulfillment requires us to embrace all that we are. The extent to which a part is disowned is the extent to which it rules us. If I can't see the part of me that pulls away from others when I get too close, then whenever I get close to another, I'll automatically pull away. If I can't see how my judgmental side always fears I'll do wrong, then I'll never take risks that put me in positions where I risk showing any incompetence.

If I can't see how tender my heart is because I'm hiding from it, then my fear of facing tender moments will rule me. Because we can't see our shadow, it unconsciously controls us. The act of owning our shadow is the act of being more conscious and therefore freer to recognize and make beneficial choices.

There is no single exercise I can offer here that would even begin to do justice to the possibilities in the Voice Dialogue system. Instead I strongly recommend you read Hal and Sidra Stone's book Embracing Ourselves, and surf the Internet to learn about resources in your area to get trained in this extraordinary system.

Authenticity and the Dance of Relationship

Often the primary reason some people feel little sense of connection is that they have built a wall of emotional protection—strong defenses that keep them from being hurt. They are guarded with others, not easily able to open up and be vulnerable. One might say that deep beneath their armoring is a tender soul who was perhaps hurt long ago, and that the armor protects that soul from being hurt again. No surprise that when that soul is healed, the armor can be released. Concurrently, when our armor is released, our soul can be revealed. The healing of our soul and the release of our armor often happen side by sid and as a result, the person becomes naturally more generous and more loving and able to be more truthful.

The experience of cutting through the armor to find our deepest truth came home to me recently in a wonderful exchange I had with a female friend, the wife of a couple my ex and I had known for years. The couple got divorced after a 20-year marriage and I maintained close contact with the husband, Bill, who is one of my best friends but not close with his ex-wife, Clara. The truth is that while I liked Clara, she and I were not close enough outside the context of the couples' friendship for me to want to keep the friendship alive, and so I did not reach out to her after the separation. A couple of years later, Clara reached out to me saying she missed our friendship, and while her relationship with her ex-husband had ended, she wanted to remain close to me. She also said she felt a sense of rejection when she had called me a couple of times and I had not responded. I told her that I had remembered the situation somewhat differently: I only recalled her calling me once, when she had requested my wife's cell phone number so she could call her (my wife and I were by then separated as well). For whatever reason, in Clara's mind she had reached out to me, and in my mind she had not.

I was a bit surprised that Clara wanted to remain friends given that she and I had not been very close. She said she was always fond of me and that she missed our connection, even though it wasn't as strong as she wanted. In response to her call, I struggled to find how to say what was true for me—that I wasn't really interested in keeping the friendship alive. While she was clearly hurting for friendship and feeling vulnerable as a newly single woman, I did not feel the reciprocal need to put energy into this friendship. So I decided to tell her the full truth—that, although I was fond of her, I wasn't inclined to reach out to her at this point. I told her this with compassion in my heart, and directness in my voice. Not surprisingly, she felt deeply hurt by my truth and asked me why I felt that way. I then explained that while we had many interactions as couples and a family, I always had difficulty getting close to her because I experienced her as guarded and often not speaking from a deep and honest place emotionally. She acknowledged that it was hard for her to allow me and others to see her most vulnerable self, and she could understand why I had that impression. I said that for me, this was the only way I wanted to be with friends and that frankly, I didn't really know her well because of what she kept hidden inside. "I care about you," I said, "and care about your well-being, and at the same time, remaining friends in the way we had been does not appeal to me. I don't have enough sense of connection to try to build on what we have, especially given that I have so many friends with whom I do have a strong connection and to whom I don't feel I give enough of my time." With sadness in her voice, she said she understood, and we bade each other a fond adieu.

Two years later, after no communications, she sent me an email saying she was deeply angry with me—that I had rejected her and left her high and dry when she was at her most vulnerable. She also reflected back what she remembered in our conversation, and much of what she remembered was very different from what I remembered or would have wanted to leave her with. Using a number of invectives, she basically told me to go to hell. I emailed her back immediately saying to her that I was deeply sorry for having contributed to her pain and that I welcomed talking and hearing more.

We spoke a few days later and the first thing out of my mouth was: "I've clearly caused you pain and suffering. I meant it when I said to you that I care about you." Her immediate response was beautiful. She said to me that she didn't feel that at all in our call two years prior. Instead, she felt "rejected and deeply hurt." Here was a woman, in contrast to how I experienced her in prior years, who was dropping down into the deepest level of her pain and sharing openly. My immediate feeling was of deep tenderness to her and sorrow for having contributed to her pain. As I felt the depth of her suffering, tears welled up in my eyes, and I said, "I am so sorry."

I explained to her again what I had felt two years ago—that I was not saying to her that I didn't care, but that it wasn't a strong enough connection to have me continue the friendship in an active way. The connection was strong enough, however, for me to hold her in my heart.

She said to me, "Keith, I can hear that and I'm completely okay with it. I guess I was so vulnerable then that all I could hear was the rejection. Not having heard from you for so long was painful for me, and our talk a couple of years ago was even more painful as you told me you didn't want to be my friend anymore. It was an incredibly hard time for me." Her voice was cracking and the vulnerable emotions were clearly present. "I'm starting to cry just thinking about how hard it's been and what I've been through."

I was deeply touched by the truth she had spoken and told her so. She told me she could now hear what she was not able to hear then and could see I was not rejecting her, but instead explaining why I had not reached back out to her. I then said that this was the most truthful I had ever experienced her and that this was the basis of the kind of friendship I seek with everyone—and that at this moment I felt closer to her than I had ever felt. She said she felt the same, and what got birthed was a deeper possibility for future friendship. We left it at that, knowing two people had just touched each other in the most intimate way imaginable.

What I take from this encounter and thousands like it is that in dropping down to our deepest truths, the ones that too often we dare not say, that magic occurs. Anything less leaves us skating the surface of life, and missing the deep wellspring from which true intimacy occurs. It is in that intimacy where both joy and sorrow are fully revealed.

You say you're angry and spit it out. I have a choice—to get defensive and shout back, or to feel the pain that causes my defensiveness and speak that truth. Underneath frustration is often unmet expectations or needs. If we could speak about our needs, then we are truly being authentic. Underneath anger is often hurt. If we could speak about the pain, then we are truly being authentic. Underneath judgment is often a feeling of threat. If we could speak about the feelings of threat, then we are being truly authentic. In the face of frustration, anger, and judgment aimed at us, we get hurt and our ego wants to protect us. The way it does is to blame, defend, and get angry and judgmental. And so the cycle continues, all under the guise of truthful communication. In the face of being told by others, however, that we are not meeting their needs, and that they are feeling hurt or threatened, our natural response is typically compassion and understanding. It is all about speaking our full truths, not just the most superficial, partial truths.

An Exercise

In the spirit of "no withholds", consider all of the areas of your life where you have a withhold—where you have a meaningful truth that you want to speak but have withheld that truth in some way. The truth could be a desire, it could be an expression of love, it could be an expression of pain or discomfort. It is whatever thought or feeling is sitting inside of you that you want to express to another but have not. Let's organize these into three fundamental categories of withholds: love, desire, and pain.

Withholding expressions of love is often a way we avoid the feeling that the other might not love us in kind. Or we fear that our communication of love might not be taken in or understood fully. Or we fear it might be misconstrued.

Withholding desire is often a way we protect ourselves from being told, "no," or being rejected. When we want something from another, it might not be given. When we don't ask, we don't know if it is a "no," so we feel safe in not asking. When we do ask, and we get a "no," we are faced with the pain of rejection. Often people who have difficulty asking for what they want don't feel they have the internal resources to face the rejection. At a deeper level is the likelihood that they are already self-rejecting, and when someone else rejects them, it's like pouring salt into a wound.

Withholding one's pain—not telling someone that you feel hurt—is often a way of not facing the potential that they won't care. Withholding the expression of pain that you feel keeps you from having to face the potential of being rejected. The young child in us can't face it, so he or she shuts down from feeling and expressing pain.

For each of these three categories (love, desire, and pain), think about three people with whom you have a withhold. For example, perhaps there is a person you feel love toward and yet withhold that expression. Or perhaps you want something but have not expressed that desire to the person or people that might be able to help you get that need met. Or you are angry and you know that underneath the anger is some hurt or pain and you know it would be healthy to acknowledge and express the pain to another person, perhaps even to the person who you sense may have triggered that pain.

Then on the left hand side of your journal, on a fresh page, name the feeling you have not expressed and on the right hand side, complete the following sentence: I withhold this expression as a way to protect myself from facing the following: _____ _____.

Naturally, you may be protecting more than one thing, so write as much as appears true to you. If it is not clear, write it as a possibility. If you are like most people, the source of your withhold will almost always be that you are afraid of the impact you will have on them, they will have on you, or the revelation will have on the relationship. By withholding you are protecting something, and your job is to find out what you are protecting. But don't take my word for it. Look deep and see if it is true for yourself. See if you can find at least 3 withholds in each of the three categories.

Consider that in all cases of a withhold there is a young and tender part of you that you are protecting. The key to expressing something that you have withheld is simple and profound. It is to own the feeling completely and not make it "about" the other. Yes, it is true that the other person is in the equation in that he or she is the object of your feeling, but your feeling is your feeling—own it as yours. You created the feeling somewhere inside of you. Others in the face of the same situation might have a different feeling. In that sense, your feeling is unique to yourself.

A Followup Exercise

In light of this, I want you to do one more thing. Take what you want to say and translate it into an expression that is purely a reflection of your own experience—something that you created. In other words, own the experience completely.

The following story involving "Diana" and "John" is a rather detailed example of how to arrive at such an expression:

Diana feels hurt by John because he doesn't take her out to dinner more often or make other overt demonstrations of love, like he used to. She translates that into the conclusion that he does not care as much as he used to. She had been sitting on this feeling for a long time, and then wrote the following:

"John doesn't seem to love me as much as he used to. I wish he would take me out to dinner, at least every now and then. I'm often the one to suggest it but I want him to. On top of that, some flowers every now and then would be nice, too. I want him to show me more often that he loves me. It hurts me that he no longer does the little things that matter in a relationship."

Note that Diana has a desire, but beneath that desire is a belief about what love is and how it should be expressed. John may love her deeply, just as much as she wants him to, but his way of expressing it may not fit her image of the way it is supposed to be expressed, or the way she prefers it to be. She believes he doesn't care and as a result feels hurt. Moreover, she has an idealized image of a man doing certain little things as a way of cultivating the relationship, but does not acknowledge that he might have (and be acting on) a different image. Her image feels universally true for her. To fully own her experience, she would need to inspect her beliefs about how love needs to be expressed and ask herself if she could feel and accept love if it were not expressed in those ways. And she would also need to acknowledge she has a belief about what fuels a relationship, and look at where that belief came from. She would likely find out that her belief is based on her preferences, and are therefore not a guide to what is true.

Once Diana explores how she formulated these theories and beliefs, she might look at different sets of beliefs she might have that would decouple her preference from what is true for John. She might consider this situation from John's point of view. She would get confirmation that John loves her deeply, and that the way he prefers to express it is by being a reliable provider. He doesn't really like his job but sticks with it day after day because it brings in earnings that allow the two of them to live a lifestyle he knows she enjoys. He feels he is sacrificing for her and that is his daily expression of love. But this expression is not tangible for Susan, because she has an image of what love should look like and feel like. By owning that she has this image, she then has the potential to see that he loves her deeply.

In your follow-up exercise, take each of the withholds that you wrote in your journal in the prior exercise and write down to its right the ways in which this feeling is one you created—in other words, a reflection of your own desires, preferences, and beliefs. Remember that in the same situation, others might react differently and have different desires, preferences and beliefs; therefore, yours are purely a result of your own inner preferences or assumptions. Perhaps the best way to do this is to write on the left hand side of the page the feeling of love, desire/need, or hurt that you are feeling. Then, on the right hand side how you created this feeling.

The Wrap-up Exercise

Now go even deeper by looking at what experiences you have owned, and ask yourself, what part of me is having this experience? (This is where Voice Dialogue is particularly instructive.) Here you are going beyond owning your own experience; you are also owning the source of that experience.

To help us here, let's revisit the Diana and John story. What was the source of Diana's experience and beliefs about love? It was an adolescent self that grew up with strong images of an idealized relationship. Perhaps it started with the way she and her friends played dolls in early childhood, then perhaps it blossomed in her teen years as she became attached to the romantic images in the movies that showed the man adoring and showering gifts on the woman. At last she began to see that society had taught her images of love that she adopted. Once owning this, she began to wonder what love might look like separate from the images she held. She went one step further and invited John to explore the same. In his exploration, John discovered that he was taking Susan for granted and that his love was once in the foreground and had slowly crept in the background. Moreover, while it felt like sacrifice to him, he realized that working in a job that he didn't like was his choice and not Susan's and that he was stuck in a paradigm that didn't fit him. This had nothing to do with Susan and all to do with the script he was living unconsciously. Together they realized each was caught in a mental construct about love and relationship that they had never questioned.

For each feeling listed in the prior exercise, write down in your journal which parts of you are the source of the belief, desire, or preference. Is it your "wounded child"? Is it an "adolescent self"? Is it your "caretaker self"—the one who always cares for others and not yourself? Is it a part of you that is highly protective of you? Consider an appropriate name for each of these parts or voices, and think about how that part created that experience. Do this for at least four of the feelings you describe earlier until the sense that you own all experiences is deeply grounded in you.

Once you have the sense that you own this experience completely, and you know from which part of you it is created, consider no longer withholding it. This is a choice. It is my view that sharing a withhold is not a good idea until you own it completely. If you don't, you may indeed face the rejection you fear. That rejection is almost always a result of expressing a feeling in a way that it is "dumped" on another. When it is dumped, the other will likely get defensive and will withdraw or attack, and so you will experience the very thing you are protecting yourself from by withholding. It is not usually the feeling that causes the reaction, but the way we hold it and express it.

What about when we are truly wronged?

Often when exploring the above, someone will take the point of view that this is all quite namby pamby. "Own what?" they might ask. "The other person is being a jerk." Fundamentally their question is: What happens when another is truly wronging me? What do we do when we are manipulated, cut down behind our backs, or any of a number of mean things that people can do to us?

My answer is simple—you still have a choice. If you feel their behavior is completely undeserved and that you are in the wake of someone who is truly trying to destroy you, then by all means, protect yourself. In the 99% of the situations that are not so clear, however, consider the possibility that the other person is simply acting out of ego protection themselves, that they are not feeling whole inside, and that it is from this place that they do damage to others and try to do damage to you. If you can truly get that, then reach out with compassion and watch their anger and attack melt away.

Another Exercise

Spend a week noticing the times when you didn't tell the truth to another. Imagine yourself tell the full truth in these moments. Write down in your journal all moments where you don't tell the truth. Include in your writing the situations, the inner feelings, thoughts, and assumptions, and any aspects that appear relevant for you. In other words, write the lie you spoke and then write any feelings, thoughts, assumptions, etc. you have about the lie.

Now look at your notes above and see if you can detect any patterns in what you have observed. Are there certain circumstances wherein you don't tell the truth? Are there certain people whom you feel you cannot or will not tell the truth to? Are there certain moments when you are particularly tender and closed in which you don't tell the truth? Write those down in your journal.

Now spend the next week telling the full truth no matter what. Be mindful of how you tell the truth so that it is offered with care in times where care is important. Be willing to offer it in a raw manner where the person or the situation will be open to your raw expression. Dance with the energies of truth-telling, but always tell the truth no matter what. I am of course referring to the meaningful truths and not the ones that seem to come and go with little to no meaning. In other words, I'm not encouraging you to blurt out anything and everything that comes to mind, just the ones that don't or won't disappear because they matter to you.

In your journal write down what it was like to tell the truth in all moments. Take particular note of the times when you ordinarily would withhold your truth. What was it like to let it out? What were the feelings, thoughts, and sensations of expressing yourself fully, unencumbered by your typical self-editing? As you write, I'd encourage you to list the hard truths you spoke and then your thoughts, feelings and assumptions about you. Keep track of these daily and then after a week see if you can detect patterns and lessons learned.

The Most Difficult Truths

The most difficult truths are the ones we have difficulty telling ourselves. We cannot speak our truth to others if we're not willing and able to speak to truth to ourselves. Our egos often protect us from seeing ourselves fully. We so wish to be seen by others as good, kind, strong and capable—and we want to see ourselves that way. We have powerful beliefs that we should be a certain ways, and with those beliefs, our ego will have difficulty in seeing anything about us to the contrary. We (or our ego) will lie to ourselves. When we behave in ways contrary to our values, we will often justify it, telling ourselves we were forced to or that any person in this situation would do this. And so we disown parts of ourselves, disbelieving or not wanting to see that they exist.

I know a man who I have experienced as incredibly inflexible. He constantly controls others and is rigidly unwilling to change or bend to meet others' needs. And yet he sees himself as quite flexible. In the face of feedback that he is often inflexible he says, "That's not true," and points out how he is simply doing what he sees as best. If he were convinced this was not the way to go, he would happily adapt. He is flexible in his own mind, in other words, as long as he is in control. He cannot seem to see himself in any other way than that of a person making intelligent decisions. The idea that he might be controlling or inflexible does not compute because he cannot admit it to himself. And, given the beautiful and ironic nature of projection, he also complains a lot when others are inflexible.

In effect, he has disowned his tendency to be inflexible and his need to control or not be controlled by others. His ego cannot see himself in any other way. Underneath this is a sense of insecurity that is so strong that he constantly tries to prove his worth to others in the form of how smart and knowledgeable he is. His insecurity reflects a weak sense of ego-self, and therefore he comes across as egotistical.

To meet and discover our deepest truths, the ones that remain hidden to us, requires that we be enormously compassionate toward ourselves. Compassion literally means loving kindness toward another ("com" = "with"; "passion" = "love"). Self-compassion simply means loving kindness toward oneself. The degree to which we feel harshly toward ourselves, beating ourselves up with self-criticism and self-loathing, is the degree to which we will not be truthful with ourselves. Parts of us, therefore, will quietly lurk in the background, acting out perceived needs without the awareness of our larger selves, until we show compassion toward ourselves and welcome each part to reveal itself. Self-compassion becomes a powerful agent for discovering all the truths of who we are, and the more we know, see, and understand ourselves, the freer we become with our choices. If I hate the part of me that is controlling, for example, it will go underground in my awareness, and yet still drive me. By being compassionate about my own controlling tendencies, I allow the awareness of control to surface such that when my need control is activated, I can see it. By seeing (rather than fearing) my need for control, my need for control is no longer automatic. In other words, when I see and own my tendencies, they no longer run me. Self-compassion, then, becomes the first and most necessary step toward self-awareness and toward a fulfilling life.

Several months ago, I felt tired and depressed, and the feelings seemed to linger for many days. It was a sense of ennui that I had never experienced before. In years past, I might have shoved these feelings aside, filling my days with activity and thus losing whatever lessons such a state might teach me. Since then, I've learned that sadness and depression can be a powerful teacher, and instead of trying to numb myself from its message, I've preferred to sink into the feeling to discover its more penetrating lessons.

As I sat with the feelings to decode their message, a thought kept coming to me. "Is this all there is?" was the voice that kept stirring in my mind. "Is there nothing more to life?" It wasn't the question that caused the sadness; it was the answer—"This is all there is." The awareness that emerged was that while I might have more experiences and highs in my life, such as a trip to France or the birth of a grandchild, I had experienced pretty much all that life would offer to me. My belief was that the only way life would be different would be to change it dramatically, and that to do so might incur a huge cost to my children, a cost that I did not want them to pay. So I felt a sense of repetition, of sameness, of being stuck in one place that was weighing heavily on me. Now don't get me wrong. I have been blessed with a rich life, filled with wonder and mystery, gains and losses, and certainly I have no desire to trade places with anyone else. And when compared to individuals stuck in highly repetitive or jobs and toxic relationships, who have never been blessed with doing (or even knowing) what their heart desires, I have little to complain about. But even a surgeon who has done complex heart surgery for 30 years can suffer from the ennui of repetition. When the feeling of "I've seen it all" emerges, it is time for a radical change.

This was the deeper truth underlying my depression—a truth I needed to face head on, without hesitation or self-judgment, or face the consequences of a deepening personal crisis. We often refer to this as a midlife crisis. Mine came later than most, perhaps because I have enjoyed such a complex life; but it came at a time when I still had major obligations to others, including two children to put through college and child-support payments—and at a time that I had finally become confidently settled in what seemed to be a career that was eminently suited to me.

I succeeded in making the requisite changes in my life, without throwing my career overboard. The changes were not, it turns out, outwardly radical, and did not need to be. Instead I have chosen to modify specific elements of my life and career so that I feel renewed. I have done that by committing to do much more writing and speaking, and much less consulting. I have also made a commitment to myself to surround myself with clients and colleagues so that I can dance the way I like to dance with clients. By choosing to work with a select few and allowing the space for more writing and speaking, my life has been altered in meaningful ways, enough so that I am filled with an ongoing sense of newness. But the particular choices I made were only the external form of the changes; they were not what was most important.

Rather, the big change in my life recently is my vow to always stop and smell the roses, no matter where I am and no matter who I am with. This inner shift has made all the difference, and ever since, my answer to the question: "Is this all there is?" has shifted. I can now answer, "No, there is so much more!" With that answer, the ennui has been lifted and has not returned ever since.

An Exercise

Write down all the feelings you have about your life in your journal. Write down the truth of your life, as you understand it. See if you can feel it in your body. Don't try to change the feelings or examine them or judge them. Just state what your life feels like now.

Now take each feeling and sense the feeling fully in your body. Note where the feeling is located, the corresponding bodily sensations, and the thoughts that arise as you feel these sensations. Don't try to change the feeling or get rid of it. Just feel it and do nothing more.

Often what we most need in our life is to simply listen, and honor what is so. When we do, our life becomes lighter and freer; things weigh us down less. It is similar to the sense of lightness achieved when someone truly hears what we feel and the oppression that accompanied the previous bottling-up of our feelings is lifted as if by magic.

You may think about this exercise as simply a great way to change or get rid of an undesirable feeling. I assure you the feeling will come back; it did not disappear forever. But this exercise is a great teacher—it shows that the more you resist a truth the more it persists, and the more you honor it, the lighter its hold on you.

CHAPTER NINE

REMEMBER: WE ARE
ALREADY CONNECTED

*"We experience ourselves, our thoughts and feelings, as something separate
from the rest — a kind of optical delusion of consciousness. This delusion is
a kind of prison for us, restricting us to our personal desires and to affection
for a few persons nearest to us. Our task must be to free ourselves
from this prison by widening our circle of compassion to embrace
all living creatures and the whole of nature in its beauty."*

– Albert Einstein

The greatest gift we can give to another is to honor their soul. The greatest connection we can experience in life is the connection borne out of an ability to touch another's heart and be touched in return. This is our final promise—to remember that we are already divine and so is everyone else, whether we are able to recognize it or not. It is the state of connection that heals all wounds, repairs all conflict, and can eradicate all war. This is not the kind of surface connection that happens fleetingly, such as when a potential lover excites us, but a pure connection that is eternal and available at any moment with anyone and any living thing. There is a wonderful story I heard many years ago, and it continues to inspire me to this day.

In days of old, a tiny group of Hebrew tribes somewhere in the heart of the country experienced months of draught, followed by disease and famine. Prior to these difficult conditions, they had enjoyed friendly and peaceful exchange among them. In their growing despair, they took to so much bickering between the villages that they ended up hating one another. Their hatred grew so fiercely that they took to fighting. Even worse, within the villages, strife mounted and neighbors began to steal from one another and spread lies. The villages were in deep turmoil.

Now beside themselves, with seemingly no way out of their troubles, the village elders from each of the tribes decided to meet to discuss what to do to stem the tide. In their discussion, it appeared that everywhere they turned there was no answer. Finally, one elder suggested they turn to the great wise one that lives in the mountains far away. Perhaps he will have the answer.

So together they marched up the mountain to seek guidance. As the great master listened to their plight, he saw the answer quite clearly. He said in a soft-spoken yet certain voice, "someone living among you is a messiah." How exciting, each thought. "And, what do we do to find him?," they asked with great eagerness. The wise man said nothing, except to assure them he is there.

With great excitement that a messiah was among them, they left to return to their villages. Upon returning, each informed their fellow villagers that the messiah lives among one of the tribes. "Where?" asked the villagers, also with great eagerness. "We don't know. We just know he is here, somewhere."

And so it began that each person looked at the other as if he or she were the messiah. They also began to look at the other tribes with whom they chanced to interact with the same respect, believing the messiah may be from there. As they greeted other people with the respect that a messiah deserves, their behavior toward one other shifted immediately. Where once there was anger and disdain, there was now gentleness, ease, grace, and a giving disposition. In each case, their gentle and generous behavior was returned in kind. Rather quickly, the sense of good will spread in and between the tribes to the point that they supported one another through what continued to be difficult conditions. Eventually, as their spirits lifted, the drought ended as well, and soon prosperity had returned.

To live in inner freedom is to recognize that you are an expression of divinity and that everyone else is as well. To see the divine in ourselves and reflected in and from the eyes of others is to experience the greatest sense of inner peace that one can find. It requires that we see past and through day-to-day petty squabbles, all the fears, feelings of threat, all the anger and judgment, and to see that underneath our remarkable differences we are all divine beings.

To live an authentic life is to care about the deeper feelings that are available in our hearts and not get distracted by emotions. Emotions are fleeting—they derive from the ego. They are reactions or interpretations of our outer world and they reside in our bodies. Inasmuch as we can change our thoughts, so too can we change our emotions.

For example, different individuals may have opposite emotional reactions to everyday occurrences—so apparently different that we tend to view the reactions as "right" versus "wrong", "proper" versus "improper." Take the case of a stranger who is trespassing on one's lawn. If that happens on Jack's lawn, Jack is greatly upset. Jack's upset may be caused by an interpretation that the lawn is his—that the stranger is on his turf without invitation and violates the sacred space that Jack has worked hard to maintain. Jack may even imagine that the stranger may cause damage to the lawn, for one who doesn't respect another's property is not likely to handle it with care. From such an interpretation, one can easily become upset and feel violated. Jack might then yell at the trespasser or just simmer in anger.

Jim has a very different interpretation of the very same act. Jim's view is that his lawn is there to be enjoyed. Jim likes that people walk on it from time to time. It is part of the larger sense of community that Jim experiences and values—part of the dance of life in which he loves to participate and have others participate. When others enter his space, Jim naturally feels ease and perhaps even pleasure. He may even greet the trespasser and end up inviting him over for conversation and refreshments.

Neither interpretation nor set of emotions and actions is "right" or "wrong." They are simply the ones that each person has. Their emotions are born out of thoughts and are quite fleeting. Interestingly, the root of the word emotion comes from the Latin word "movere" which means to move. Emotions are not at all fixed or static; they move.

Deeper feelings, by way of contrast, are not of the mind and ego, but of the heart, and have a much more enduring quality. They tend to be softer in nature. They are rooted in the soul, and are uncondi-tional—not dependent on mood or circumstance. Nevertheless, these feelings visit us more at some times than others. We all have moments when these deep feelings come to the fore, and then we recognize a qualitative difference in how we perceive and live life. In those times we recognize that a quiet centeredness, effervescent joy, a still mind, and a compassionate, open heart reflect our true self. When connected to our deeper feelings and a more enduring way of being, unconditional love and simple pleasure are native and natural to us.

The key to making this profound recognition more constant and less the exception is remembering that all of us are already connected. The capacity to love and be loved is available in each of us and only requires that we remember to open our hearts and feel the connection that is ever present.

To understand what I mean, let's explore the nature of giving.

Types of Giving

I believe there are four different types of giving, each emanating from different parts of our selves. First is the giving that is a form of taking in disguise. It often comes in a way that seems to say, "Let me give so I can impress you with my giving nature." Businesses and business people sometimes do this to advertise something they are not. The recent advertisements from many companies that are notorious polluters of the environment claiming they are committed to a sustainable planet have the general smell of something like this. Another way this particular form of giving shows up is by giving in front of others so they adore us for the fact that we give. In this type, our giving is designed consciously or unconsciously to get something—to prove to others that we are givers. In so doing, we are giving to get something.

The second type of giving is to give because we are supposed to. Many people give out of obligation or duty. They were taught that one should give—their values dictate it. It is hard for me to describe the difference between this kind of giving and a more pure one, for one could easily argue it is pure—I value giving so I give. To me this type of giving can feel empty and transactional in nature when obligation is the primary impetus. One can give from value or obligation and then check off the box. The exchange of boundless love that is available between giver and receiver does not quite happen when done out of obligation. Gratitude from the receiver may show up, as might satisfaction on the part of the giver, but the delicious comingling of eternal love-—the feeling of total non-separation from each other and non-separation from the source of our being—may be lacking.

The third type is giving with the knowledge it will be reciprocated. It is giving with an expectation of something offered in return. We make deals with the people in our circle, often tacitly, sometimes explicitly. I will do this for you, but you do something for me in return. Giving becomes more of social exchange, born out of the desire to get, or out of a limited image of fairness. It, too, lacks the deliciousness of pure giving and pure receiving.

The final type of giving is giving out of love with no expectation of something to be given in return. It is giving with no desire for attention, appreciation, or recognition. It is pure giving and it is the rarest kind, for it comes out of pure love of others and a strong sense of connection to all and everything—it comes from our sense of divinity. Interestingly, the people who give from this place don't need to get anything, for their love is boundlessly deep and they feel complete with that love.

Remember a time when you gave fully and freely, with no expectation. Remember how you felt. You were present with that person or people. Your heart was boundless in that moment, and you loved the experience of giving. Your love for that person or people in that moment was pure, and the light in your eyes, the beaming smile on your face, and the tenderness in your heart showed it fully. You felt connected to that person and needed nothing from them. You were living out the purest definition of charity as quoted below from the New Testament's First Letter of Paul to the Corinthians, chapter 13.[14] Take note of the clear reference to fleeting experience of emotions born out of egoistic desires. You can see the call to a more enduring relationship to giving that can only come from living deep from within our hearts.

If I speak in the tongues of mortals and of angels, but do not have love, I am a noisy gong or a clanging symbol. And if I have prophetic powers, and understand all mysteries and all knowledge. And if I have all faith, so as to remove mountains, but do not have love, I am nothing. If I give away all my possessions, and if I hand over my body so that I may boast, but do not have love, I gain nothing.

Note that Saint Paul is saying that although I am many powerful things, I am nothing without true love. I could be extraordinary in my giving, but if that giving does not come from true love), it is empty. The author goes on to speak in a way that distinguishes true love from the other forms of giving expressed above.

Love is patient; love is kind; love is not envious or boastful or arrogant or rude. It does not insist on its own way; it is not irritable or resentful; it does not rejoice in wrongdoing, but rejoices in the truth. It bears all things, believes all things, hopes all things, endures all things.

In this passage, Paul is saying that giving from love is pure and as a result is deeper and beyond all other things. Note, by the way, that in older versions of the bible, it is referred to in these passages as "charity." In my view, this suggests the powerful connection between true and pure charity, and love.

In a similar way to what St. Paul states, I suggest that the first three types of giving discussed above are not pure giving at all. They look like giving, but because they are partial forms, they lack the fullness of what giving truly is. Put another way, they lack the spirit of true giving, which is to give freely and fully, with no expectation of anything. When giving is offered in part, the receiver of that giving experiences a hook of some kind and so he or she receives it carefully or reluctantly.

We feel it in our bodies when the giving is not pure, just as we feel it in our bodies when it is pure. Arguably, deep within, we are all generous. We all have a tender and giving heart. Giving and receiving become as one in the context of feeling a connection. If you and I are not separate, but connecting in the vast stream of life, then as I give to you, so too do I naturally receive, for you and I are one and the same. Giving in the transactional sense comes from ego—a sense that I am separate and must take care of me/mine. Giving in this more purse sense comes from a sense of connection.

But it is our wounding and the armor that protects us that prevent us from expressing that loving nature. When we feel safe with others, we give more. Put differently, it is the nature of a part of us (our loving self, or soul) to give, and it is the nature of another part of us (our ego) to not give. The less tender the wound or the less bounded the armor, the less encrusted the ego, the more likely we will give.

And the greatest gift we can offer to others is not of material things, although those can be sweet. It is the gift of full acceptance—of loving a person as they are, with no expectations that they be any different. It is the gift of honoring their soul.

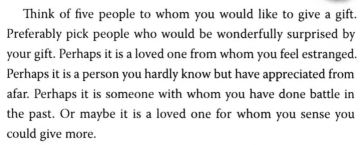

An Exercise

Think of five people to whom you would like to give a gift. Preferably pick people who would be wonderfully surprised by your gift. Perhaps it is a loved one from whom you feel estranged. Perhaps it is a person you hardly know but have appreciated from afar. Perhaps it is someone with whom you have done battle in the past. Or maybe it is a loved one for whom you sense you could give more.

Now think of each person and imagine a gift that would truly be a gift for him or her. For example, when my daughter was 9, I gave her a full day of my uninterrupted time. We played, danced, went to the movies, played some more, snuggled and read together (I told her a story when I put her to bed). The next day, as I dropped her off to her mom's, she gave me the biggest and tightest hug I could ever remember and offered words that are so delicious to my ears, "I love you daddy." It was because it was her day and not mine that the gift had such an impact.

Pick a gift and allow yourself to feel your love for the other person. Or let whatever feelings of tenderness emerge, no matter how lofty or subtle. Then give the gift, with absolutely no strings attached. As you give it, feel the love you have of this person, of yourself, and of all humanity. Feel and sense that person's—and everyone's—divine nature. Truly allow yourself to be touched as you offer it. And then do nothing more. Afterwards, note in your journal what it felt like to give it and what moved you at each step along the way.

To know as I am known, to touch another as I am touched, to be as I am in the deepest sense of who I am and to support others to do the same, is the greatest glory available to human creation. Paraphrasing Rumi, our soul is here for its own joy, and when we take care of our deepest self—our soul—we feel expansive, giving, honoring, and a natural sense of love for the world around us. This has been referred to as agape love. Agape love, in the sense that I mean it, is not the love one might feel for a spouse or a lover, but the love one feels for all and everything. It is available to all, but only when we drop down into our body, and especially into our heart, and experience a deep and abiding sense of connection—from one soul to another.

The best way I know to live and experience the pleasure of living in and from our soul is to love another purely as they are—to remember that in our heart of hearts we are all connected and that each person is a unique expression of their soul's desire. If we could do that, and invite others to join us, then we would find heaven on earth, and every form of strife—from interpersonal relationships to wars—would naturally melt away.

On the Folly of Molding Others

I'm sitting by the side of a large circular fire pit a group of us dug at Dillon Beach, on the coast of Northern

California. The pit is about eight feet in diameter, and
in it are about 40 pieces of pottery shared among seven
or eight of us. The fire is now smoldering and beginning
to cool, and as it does, I wait eagerly to see how my
nine pieces have turned out, as do all the others. We
have devoted many hours to creating our pots and are
full of anticipation as to how they will come out. Will
they be cracked? How will the dance of the fire have
impacted them? Will they be magnificent or ordinary?

The process by which we do the pit fire is a powerful metaphor for life and a powerful learning tool for me. I used to throw pots and glaze them. The glazes came out okay, but I was constantly frustrated that the glaze ran, dripped, or did not come out in the way I imagined. That is often true for me in life. I have images of what I want and try to control life so that it fulfills my image. Often I've been disappointed.

But in the past few years I've given up trying to create pottery exactly to the specifications in my mind. I've discovered that it is a rather futile effort—just as is the effort to control life. Life does not seem to want to conform to what I want, so I end up unsatisfied and often frustrated. I believe my early parenting style was driven by a desire to control the destiny and growth patterns of my son—to mold him into some image that would make me proud. I know I'm not alone. Many parents feel the same. I'm actually pretty good at getting what I want in life and in having images and then manifesting those images. In other words, like others I fairly often get what I want, but to do so is a fleeting satisfaction that only feeds my ego's belief that I am powerful. And when I don't get what I want, my ego is often upset, my mind racing to fix the problem and bend the world to my will. Funny how the world does not so quickly bend! The same is true of the pots I've thrown and glazed. Some come out consistent with my images, most not. And the more attached I've become to those images and outcomes, the more unsatisfactory the experience.

Pit firing for me feels more congruent with how I now see life. The process is simple and quite profound. After forming our pots in whatever forms we choose or are capable of, we burnish them to create a shiny surface. We then bisque-fire them to about 1300 degrees, less than the heat needed for glazed pots, but enough to harden the clay. We dig a rather large and deep pit on the beach, surround the insides with metal to keep the sand from falling into the pit, toss a layer of sawdust at the bottom, and gently place our pots in the sawdust. Later, the sawdust smolders under the flames, and the lack of oxygen creates a blackened area on the pots. We then sprinkle carbon carbonate and salt and seaweed around the pots, the fumes from which cause swirling images of red and gentle yellow. We place dry cow dung on the pots to encourage slow cooling and also to provide a bit of yellow or light brown. After we carefully cover the pots with a lot of wood, we light the fire. It is quite a spectacle as it burns powerfully, the smoke, fumes and fire imprinting their uncontrollable and yet guidable messages.

At best, all we can do is guide the process. We have a sense of what we want, but only that. And then we release our desires to the fire gods, seeking not to control the outcome but instead to experience the wonder of its own internal beauty. Similarly, at best all we can do in life is to guide it gently. Like the metal boundaries that protect the pots from the sand falling into them, we form boundaries for protection. Beyond that, life wants to unfold as it does, and our interventions to try to control it are sheer folly. It is when I allow the full expression of life to imprint me—when I find myself dancing with the flames—that I at last begin to live life with joy, fluidity, and a sense of awe.

We now sit and wait for the pots to cool. We are all eager in anticipation. We must wait, patiently. If we take our pots out too soon, the coolness of the air against the heat of the pot will cause it to crack. Even the cracks are a powerful message. Often, the pots will have tiny fissures. They can be reminders of our beautiful imperfections. When the pots crack fully and are ruined, it is a reminder that life, like art, is quite fragile, and often we just need to let go completely of the outcome and simply love the process. This has been a powerful challenge to me in my life. It teaches me that "failure" is as natural and necessary as "success," and that acceptance of what is, letting go, and moving on are of a higher order of wisdom than the unnatural and unrealistic expectation that our lives should be a string of pure "successes." To an artist's mind, failure is an incomparable teacher and feedback mechanism; it forces us to strive for more profound and true successes than we had previously dreamed. Above all, failure is a lesson in letting go.

As I've gone through the journey of life, I spent most of my youth and young adult life trying to mold myself to become the person my parents wanted me to become. I worked hard and did not enjoy much of my growing-up years. Instead of just playing, I was always concentrating on meeting my internalized hand-me-down expectations.

In my early adulthood, I was committed to being the best consultant I could be. I worked hard and honed my skills, and eventually became one of the best in my field. And yet my life felt disturbingly unsatisfying. I was neither truly happy nor depressed, but simply driven, rarely stopping to enjoy the inherent wonder of life itself. As I moved toward middle age, I began to see that all of my early ambitions were a young person's desire to get the love I wanted from my parents. If only I would become the person they wanted me to be, then they would be proud and love me.

Now that I am squarely in "middle age," I realize that the chase to achieve great things was rather hollow. What I have begun to want from life is to simply drink its pleasures. This communion with life itself is my soul's deeper desire, rather than fulfilling any predefined dreams. To do this, I have had to listen to the whispers of my soul rather than the cacophony of my upbringing and cultural expectations. I have had to interpret my soul's quiet but powerful message. Like the pots in the pit whose swirls are images of beauty and grace, my life is at last unfolding along its own course, guided by my ability to listen, undisturbed by my ego's desire to control. And now, more than ever, I see that others have their own path, and their journey unfolds in their own time and at their own pace. My job is not to control my own life or others' lives, but to bask in the glory of its unfolding.

Fritz Perls, a leader of the gestalt therapy movement in the 1960s and an icon of humanistic psychology, said it clearly in his simple poem:

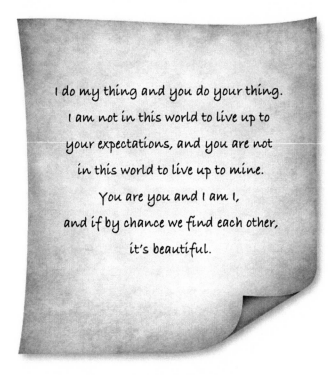

I do my thing and you do your thing.
I am not in this world to live up to
your expectations, and you are not
in this world to live up to mine.
You are you and I am I,
and if by chance we find each other,
it's beautiful.

In simple language, this poem evokes a great truth. My job is to discover my own soul's code and honor its message. Yours is to do the same. Our collective job is to respect each other for our own truth.

Power Over Versus Power With

There are fundamentally two expressions of power in the world—power over, and power with. Power over others is the tendency to want to dominate—to take control and mold others in our own image. Power over others is the tendency to dictate to others how they should or will be. At the extreme, war is an expression of such a desire. My life, my belief, my religion, my ways of being is right, and my job is to get you to live consistent with them. People will kill others in the service of such a belief. That is power over.

Power with others is the desire to collaborate—to take my know-how and my gifts and meld them with yours to form a great synergy—something more than either of us could create alone or even imagine. It stems from the belief that differences are mutually complementary and empowering, and that there is greater potential in life when fresh and different energies come together. Differences invite learning, exploring, and the potential for deepening. When we each take our unique gifts and our unique expression of such gifts and seek to collaborate, a new whole begins to materialize in front of us as if by magic.

Simply put, people who live authentically—who are fully comfortable with who they are—have no need for power over others. They honor and treasure differences. They seek to dance with life and know that the dance is richer when it is more varied. Differences beget challenges and unfold new, wondrous realities.

Picture two people on a tour bus to a foreign and very different country. One keeps seeing the people through his or her own eyes and judges their behavior based on set values. "They shouldn't do this or that," "Ooh, that's gross," "How could they...?" are all words that come from this person's mouth. At the extreme, this is the archetypal "Ugly American" who believes our culture's behavior is right, that we are the best, and therefore others are wrong or inferior. The other person, in contrast, gets out of the bus with deep curiosity and a sense of wonder. "Oh my, how fascinating," "That's extraordinary," "I'd love to find out more about these people" are words that come from this person's mouth.

The first person is expressing the thoughts and feelings that arise out of the felt need for power and control over others. In its extreme manifestations, this can lead to programs to eradicate a culture or convert individuals to the prevailing culture, religion, or nationalistic loyalties. The second person sees him- or herself as a learner, with no agenda or judgment to impose—and differing forms of expression are a source of delight and wonder. That person will experience great joy in the trip, while the first will only end up with souvenirs and righteous indigna-tion. The path of power with others creates possibilities and synergies far beyond the capability of individuals alone. This path emanates from an awareness of and respect for our mutual connectedness—a realiza-tion that together we are far stronger and more fulfilled than apart. The path of power over others, in contrast, creates corruption, decay, strife, an atmosphere of mutual threat, and an insatiable need for more and more control over others.

An Exercise

Consider the subtle or not-so-subtle ways in which we express power over another. One such moment in my life describes the subtlety and pervasiveness of this need to have power over another. I was talking with a woman with whom I was explor-ing a romantic relationship one day, and I asked her how she felt about some particular thing (which I can no longer remember). I only remember the words I uttered as she paused for about ten seconds to consider her answer to my question. I said, "Take your time." The literal meaning of these words—which mean, in effect, "No need to rush on my account. I'm patient"—would not seem to pose a problem. (If I had indicated impatience, wouldn't that have been worse?) But her response revealed a subtext to what I was saying. She said firmly and clearly, "I will." There was a bit of fierceness in her voice—not so much defensiveness as an inner clarity. Her words and tone were telling me, "You don't need to tell me to take my time. I am comfortable in my skin and need no permission from you." It was quite instructive to notice that in a subtle way, I had put myself in a one-up position related to her, and she would have none of it. When we grant permission to others (whether asked for or not), we are involved in one-upsmanship. It assumes one has the power to grant a choice to another—or that they need our permission to respond in a cer-tain way. In truth, we have no such power—and they do not need our permission—but we often act as if this were the case. And that is exactly what I was doing in this moment. In reflecting on this, I wondered about the many ways I do that—such as saying, "you might want to consider...", or "I wouldn't do that," or more overtly, "that's just wrong."

These are all moments where I am putting myself in a position to judge, and in so doing taking a one-up position in relationship to the other. Giving unsolicited advice is a particularly interesting example of one-up behavior because it looks so giving on the surface. But deeper down there is a message of "I know something you don't know." The advice-giver unconsciously or consciously believes the receiver does not have the inner strength, know-how, or wherewithal to address the problem on her own. Hence giving unsolicited advice is a one-up position.

Think of the myriad ways in which you put yourself in a one-up position relative to others. Write those down on the left hand side of your journal. Now, think about the message you are sending that person in taking this stance, and write your thoughts on the right hand side.

To live life from a power with mentality versus a power over mentality has much to do with being authentically and fully expressed and in supporting others to do the same. When your desires, aims and beliefs are shared, then mutual support is both possible and welcome. When they are not, the best we can do is honor and respect the different paths.

I believe that all wars are caused by an inability to live this way. We believe our way is the right way and so we try to impose it on others. We believe our relationship to God or our way of life is the right one and so we proselytize. We believe our beliefs are the right beliefs and so we let others know how wrong they are. Out of a deep insecurity and a deep need to dictate how others live, we engage in all kinds of wars. Sometimes those wars are fought with guns. Other times they are fought with words. Each is the same. I am right; you are wrong. And my job is to tell you so, convince you, and impose (even force) my view on you.

If we embrace who we are, we have no "need" to impose our beliefs or lifestyle on others. And if we are secure in ourselves, we give others the space to be themselves, so we have no reason to exercise power or control over them. The joy of following one's own muse is only enhanced when others are following their own muse as well.

When a person lives their life fully and authentically, they are imbued with enormous power. It is not the power assigned by position or by edict from another powerful source (such as the a king giving knighthood to a person), it is the source of personal power. When the Romans asked Jesus by whose authority he spoke his words, he declared "by my own authority." People who live their own heart's desire have their own intrinsic authority. This is the only kind of authority that cannot be taken away, for it was never bestowed on them in the first place, but arose spontaneously and integrally from the depth of their being. This kind of authority represents inner freedom at its fullest.

At age 56, I believe I have finally figured out the key to fulfillment. It is not in living a life defined by my parents, my community, nor the society that surrounds me. It is living my soul's deepest desire fully and unabashedly. It took me a long time to figure it out, and for the past ten years my life has been bending ever more toward the compass of my soul. In each curve I have found greater and greater satisfaction, to the point that for the first time in my life, I'm able to dance with life and bask in its own pleasure. Rumi's statement that the soul is there for its own joy describes how I see the life in front of me. I can never know exactly the path ahead of me, but if I listen carefully, my true path will progressively unfold.

Too often we look at another person's behavior and judge it, either positively or negatively. Regardless of the valence of the judgment, it comes from the same belief and the same source. We believe—or, put more accurately, a part of us believes—it is our right to dictate or define another person's life. Just as we have inherited these beliefs about ourselves, we also have formed beliefs about what others should or should not do. And we believe it is certainly within our right to express those beliefs.

To the extent that we believe we're living a correct and appropriate life and we have some need for others to act consistent with ourselves, we will tell others what they're doing right or wrong in life. We forget that we're all different; instead, we believe our success strategies are universally true.

The source of judgment runs much deeper. Once you get the source, you will see all judgments as opportunities to deepen your own capacity to live life consistent with your deepest heart's desire.

An Exercise

Go back to your list of one-up actions and consider what you might have done in the same circumstance had you felt completely at ease with yourself and held the other person in complete regard. From that place, what would you have done or not done differently? What would have been the effect? What message would you be sending by your alternative stance in the matter? Write your thoughts in your journal next to each time you took a one-up stance.

The Source of All Negative Judgments

A negative judgment is simply the act of believing that what another person is doing is wrong—that they should be doing something different. A judgment is different from an assessment. Making assessments is crucial to an effective life. We face situations all the time where we need to determine which direction to go, what will likely work or not work, which action will serve our goals, and the like. These are acts of discernment that are much needed. Judgments are not needed, except for our own ego protection.

An Exercise

Before we lift the veil to discover the source of our negative judgments, I invite you to do an experiment. For the next few days, whenever you experience yourself judging another, write in your journal the following:

1. What is the content of the judgment?

2. What are the underlying beliefs, biases, or assumptions about the person or that person's behavior?

3. What does your judgment remind you of in your past?

4. How does that person's behavior threaten you (your well-being, your beliefs, your livelihood, etc.)?

In doing this exercise with hundreds of people, I have discovered that almost all judgments are targeted toward behaviors that threaten us psychologically and that the ultimate source of our judgments is our lack of inner solidity. The more you are solid with yourself the less you will judge others. Simply put, you can spend your life judging others and trying to mold others to behave in a way that you deem safe and comfortable, or you can develop your own inner solidity and enjoy the pleasure that differences in behavior offer to us all.

The more we are solid with ourselves and live our own life, the easier it is to support others in doing the same. With inner solidity, we have no need to mold others, for we don't experience others as a threat. Instead their differing views and behaviors add richness to the dance of life and we take pleasure in joining in its movement.

Positive Judgments

The act of positively judging another is simply the belief that others' actions or behaviors are right or good. It is assigning a positive valence to them or their behavior. Its source is the same as negatively judging, although we are fine with people offering positive judgments of us and are hurt when they form negative ones. In either case, positive or negative, it is driven by a belief that people should live consistent with a certain image or set of rules. To the extent that you, I, or anyone are positively judging, we are saying, in effect, "I like it when you behave consistent with the image that I have. If you do, I will then not be threatened." Positive judgments, then, are simply a way to avoid the feeling of threat.

Parenting an Authentic Child

Perhaps the hardest test of the philosophy of authenticity is how we raise our children. Do we parent our child in a way that supports his or her natural unfolding? Our parents' efforts to mold us were largely driven by a need to have us conform to the unwritten rules of society—rules that they had assimilated and reflexively needed to pass on to us. If we behaved outside those norms, they feared they would be negatively judged, so they worked hard to be sure we lived rightly. Their efforts to mold us were also driven by a belief about what a good person is. Our parents had images of what we should be in terms of our livelihood, with a sense that if we became that, we would do them proud. By your behaving consistent with their image of the good, they could say to the world, "Take a look at what I've created."

By molding you, they were unconsciously trying to prove to themselves and the world around them that they are good parents. In recent generations, goodness came to be defined in terms of what you did, not who you are. Of course, patterns of parenting differ widely, but very few of us (and very few of our children) escaped the effects of society's push toward status. And the more the child achieves a high status, as evidenced by education, intellect, power, prestige, and earning power, the better the parent.

And so our parents had many conscious and unconscious rules about right living, and they did their best to mold us consistent with these rules. We learned that this is what good adults do—they tell others what they should or should not do. This is how we learned to relate to others early on in life, and so we pass it on.

Since nearly all of us were parented in this way, we in turn tend to follow suit, not questioning the underlying assumptions behind our own parenting. In my view, the act of parenting at its best is not molding a child at all. It is being curious about, creating (or allowing) an environment for, and reveling in the natural expression of the child. Of course boundaries must be set, especially early on, but the more the child is encouraged to find their own voice and discover the shape of their own life, the more satisfaction the child will have in life.

Each step we take is a choice in life. And even more so, how we step, where we come from internally as we step, is a choice. Do I live life from my personality, letting desires, preferences, or reactions shape my moment-by-moment existence? Do I live from ego, protecting myself, seeing myself as separate? Do I follow the dictates of my community, my family, or others around me, thereby falling into the comfortable embrace of conformity? When we make life choices and relate to others from these places, there is a consequence—we shrivel inside, little by little. Worse, we can't tell it's happening. When we parent from the same place, we restrict life from unfolding fully and naturally. How we parent is an expression of who we are and, more deeply, how we parent ourselves. So the ultimate question is: do I have the courage to take the step to live from my deepest core—from my soul and my divinity—and thereby experience greater joy and inner freedom than I ever imagined possible?

CHAPTER TEN

CREATING AN
AUTHENTIC LIFE

*"I would rather be ashes than dust! I would rather that my spark should
burn out in a brilliant blaze than it should be stifled by dry rot. I would rather
be a superb meteor, every atom of me in magnificent glow, than a sleepy
and permanent planet. The proper function of man is to live, not to exist.
I shall not waste my days in trying to prolong them. I shall use my time."*

– Jack London

To live a full and passionate life, a life that takes us to a place of inner
freedom, requires enormous courage. It requires that we take a stand
and risk ridicule and failure. It requires that we live vulnerably, willing
to face the potential for enormous pain and at the same time, inviting
the potential for enormous joy. And most importantly, it requires that
we distinguish between our fleeting emotions and our deeper soul's
knowing. Getting to inner freedom requires no less than the ability to
let go of ego and the fears from which it derives and live from a place
of true wisdom.

How can we discover and come to terms with the forces in us that
keep us from living authentically? As we've discovered, it requires
a process of observation and listening. Recently, I was talking with a
client about the challenges she was facing finding her purpose. In the
course of our conversation, all of the sudden, she got clear about her
purpose. "It's about imaginative communication," she said with a gusto
that showed she was on to something meaningful. As she continued
speaking, I could see her body come alive as I'd never seen before. She
was clearly lit up. This, as we've seen, is a sign that one is on to something in the arena of soul and purpose. When I reflected back to her

what I had heard and seen, she because immediately quite shy, as if being seen in all of her glory was not okay with some part of her.

This was an important moment. Shyness can be a powerful teacher, and I clearly saw it the moment it emerged. "Are you aware you just got quite shy?" I asked gently. "Yes, I can feel it," she replied, appreciating that she was being seen in all ways, not just the glory of her purpose. "Let's feel into that shy part and see what it may reveal."

In the course of our exploration, she could see both the part of her that is her soul and the part that puts shackles on it. She was afraid to be seen so fully. Such is often the case. One can feel extraordinarily vulnerable when expressing one's purpose, because one never knows if something of such undeniable personal value will be validated by others—or if one will appear a fool to the outside world, or even be rejected for saying it. Sometimes what is most sacred to oneself seems to need special protection from the assaults of doubt from others. Consider how it feels when someone scoffs at our dreams; although their action may seem harmless, the effect is to trample on our soul. When we experience this so much in life, it is no wonder our soul goes underground, unwilling and unable to be seen even by ourselves, let alone expressed in the world.

As my client and I continued, we examined what her shyness revealed about what must be guarded and what must be tended to in order for her purpose to be expressed, until she was able to safely affirm her soul's purpose to herself and to others.

The contemporary poet Javan has given us a taste of inner freedom as well as its attendant vulnerability in his poem, "Maybe I Will Never Be."

I'm not very good at this Game called Life
For I've not learned to see children crying
Without feeling pain.

For I've not learned to watch animals destroyed
Without wondering why.

For I've not yet met a king or a celebrity
that I would bow down to
or a man so insignificant
that I could use for a stepping-stone.

For I've not learned to be a 'yes man'
to narrow minded bosses who quote rules without reason.
And I've not learned to manipulate the feelings of others,
to be used for my own advantages then cast aside as I see fit.
No, I'm not very good at this Game called Life.
And if everything goes well,
Maybe I never will be.

– Javan (1984)

I recently received a phone call from a friend of mine, Sheryl, who was frantic with concern. Just before the call, my body was calm. I felt centered and present—centered in that the locus of my energy was near my belly; present in that my attention was in the present moment. In that space, there was nothing to do, nowhere to go. I remained calm as Sheryl told me frantically about a highly volatile situation in a community of which we are both a part. I wanted to ask questions to clarify the issues, but there was no room to get my questions in—her presentation was a nonstop maelstrom of fear. And so I listened, without interrupting her.

As Sheryl spoke, I was able to visualize all of the forces that conspired to create this present mess in our community. I allowed these images to flow through, including an image of our community sitting on the precipice of a disaster. As this image began to form, I could feel fear quickly arising inside of me—the very same fear she was exhibiting. Fortunately, I was awake enough to the present moment to notice that it was a story I'd made up, encouraged by Sheryl's story. As the fear washed over me, I let it melt away as quickly as it came—and it was replaced by a deeper sense of trust of myself and of my ability to navigate treacherous waters. This deeper sense of trust allowed me to become calm once again.

Finally, she asked, "What should we do?" In the inner circle of my calm, I spoke honestly: "I don't know, at least not yet."

"Aren't you concerned?" she asked with more than a bit of curiosity, noticing my calm in the face of her storm. "I am a bit," I replied honestly. "I care about this community deeply and yet at the same time I trust we'll figure it out."

Sheryl started to calm down, sensing my inner certainty. It was a certainty not born out of cognitive clarity about what to do. Rather, it was born out of a trust in my ability to allow the ebbs and flows of emotions and to be curious about their source—my own thoughts. It was born out of knowing that thoughts are fleeting and that wisdom comes from a different pool. It was born out of the capacity to let go of ego for a moment and to listen to my intuition. It was born out of a capacity to be curious and not land on a conclusion until all was explored. It was born out of a clear distinction between immediate reactions and wise responses.

I invited her to join me here, in this place of exploration, knowing that when she did we would together figure out how to best respond. I offered her a bit of feedback. "You seem a bit frantic." These words tumbled out of my mouth with warmth and compassion. They were not a judgment of her, but simply a description, said with genuine empathy.

"I am," she replied honestly. "I think the viability of our community is at stake." She wove me a tale of a potential future that demonstrated how this particular crisis could quickly snowball into a true catastrophe. I could feel some fear rising in me once again, like a gentle wave moving up my torso following the images of disaster rattling in my head.

"Sheryl," I said with conviction, "I can see how this might happen. I can also see how we'll figure out how to meet this moment in a way that prevents it from happening. The future is very much a question and how we respond matters a lot."

I added gently, "We won't be able to figure it out from the place of fear." Sheryl nodded. "Yes, I know," she said in a deeper, calmer voice, suggesting that the fear, born out of her thoughts, was beginning to melt away. She was ready to join me now in a dance of exploration that had the potential to stem the tide. Such an exploration required us both to access a deeper sense of knowing that is often best accessed in stillness.

I suggested a way to get there. "Let's both take a few breaths and sense the place inside ourselves where we know we'll be able to figure out what to do."

After about a minute or so in which we calmed our minds through our breath and entered this deeper source, we began to explore how our community had created its own crisis and what we might do to support them to get out of it. To the extent that there were many others involved, we knew we couldn't control the situation or the behaviors of others.

Once our strategy was complete, we put it into effect. Days later, there was much learning and a disaster was diverted. Through it all, I felt many emotions. I felt some fear, a great deal of trust, and a strong dose of my own capacity to remain centered and calm amidst a swirl of anxiety among others. I did not stuff any of these emotions, nor did the emotions take over. I swam fluidly in the waters of uncertainty and invited her to join me—neither fighting the currents nor being swept by them. Situations like this can be very valuable, for they teach us how our sense of what is real and possible is limited or distorted by our automatic fear-based responses. In these situations, even our sense of what is logical or inevitable is skewed by our emotions. Simply recognizing our emotional state for what it is can be the first big step toward inner freedom. In addition to this recognition, calming our bodies and minds can help us achieve inner clarity and become open and receptive to possibilities that we may not have considered. All of life has the fluidity of a dance. In terms of the mind, such fluidity includes inquisitiveness about oneself, others, and the situations one is in—a far cry from the fearful, frozen fatalism that is our common reaction. It is never a matter of controlling life, nor of allowing life to overtake one. It means neither reacting, nor acting precipitously. And it requires truth telling, at all points and in all meaningful ways.

I was playing golf alone on a beautiful Saturday, the day before Christmas. Few people were out on the course, and I was enjoying the scenery and the experience of being alone without a care—just me, the golf ball, and the course, nothing more. About half way through the course I became aware that for nine holes, I was playing careful golf, trying hard to do well. My score on the first nine was decent, but not spectacular by any means. And then an image came to mind. What if I could swing free and easy, without concern as to where the ball fell? What if I could swing unencumbered by the concern as to whether it was close to my aim or not, whether I had blown it or not blown it? Held by this thought, I took a couple of practice swings, just loose and easy. I then formed an image in my mind, not of where I wanted the ball to go, but how I wanted to feel in my swing—and then I swung the club. It was the best shot I'd ever hit in my life—a 5 iron from 190 yards. It landed two feet from the hole. And then I smiled, not so much from the result, which was indeed sweet in and of itself, but from the exquisitely light sensation of being free of care. At that instant I realized that for most of my life of golf, I had been playing careful golf--golf so full of care that I was overly controlling of my swing. My body would be wound up so tight up that the swing was stiff, lacking the languor and fluidity that a good golf shot needs.

That wonderful image of carefree golf stayed with me for the rest of the holes as I played the most spectacular nine holes of my life. Two other shots were the finest, sweetest, easiest shots I had hit as long as I can remember. One ended up on the 13th tee for a hole in one. For a lover of golf this is a rare event. Most golfers golf their whole life without one. In that moment, I felt blessed.

As I reflected on the experience later, I realized that not only had I played golf overly filled with care, but that I played life the same way. I was more concerned with avoiding failure than with living life, free of constraint. That experience and my later reflections gave birth to a distinction that has since taken hold in my awareness—the difference between a carefree life, a careful life, and a careless life. Too often we go through life between two extremes. At one end, we play life too carefully, wanting to conform, wanting to show up in a way that others would not disapprove of or that we wouldn't disapprove of, and thus depriving ourselves of a life that is driven by our soul's purpose. At the other extreme, we may live a careless life, not caring about who we are and how we express life, not caring about others. And, in our carelessness, we play sloppy. We hurt others unintentionally. We hurt ourselves, not allowing ourselves the joy of passionate, purposeful living. Life instead should be lived in freedom—responsively, fluidly, expressively, lovingly (to others and to ourselves). To live life in such a way means I allow others to also be free to express their soul—free to live their life fully.

It's really not about creating such a life, in the sense of planning a project. It's more about discovering and supporting that which wants to be. Once your purpose is discovered, you will likely find many ways of expressing this purpose, and in so doing, you will feel lit up by life. There will be many paths that will get you there, and deciding which path to choose may sometimes be difficult. I have found in my life that the expression of my purpose has changed while my purpose has not. Instead of drifting from career to career, my career has morphed as my talents and interests have evolved. Similarly, my values have not changed much, but I have become much less rigid in terms of how they are expressed in the world. In other words, where once I lived by rigid rules of conduct, now I live within flexible principles. As I've loosened my grip on what a "right" life looks like, I find myself much more flexible around people who look and act very different from me. With inner clarity comes less of a tendency to control others or life, and less of an expectation that things will always present themselves in a certain way.

They key to manifesting one's purpose is not so much in the planning, although planning may be helpful. The key is in the choosing. To live one's own life is a courageous choice, one not for the faint of heart. It is a choice to be true to yourself, and be willing to let go of relationships of the past and society's definitions of success. It is a choice to follow one's soul. It is a choice to care more about spiritual, social and emotional health than financial wealth. It is certainly possible to achieve it all, but if financial wealth and security are most important to you, then your soul will remain stuck to the ground while your ego tries to soar. I have found that to live a fulfilling and gratifying life, the soul has to take center stage, and in so doing, you become more capable and more effective. As a result you get good and even great at what you love to do, and money often naturally follows as a byproduct, but it is not your primary goal.

Nevertheless, some of you readers will try to slip the goal of wealth acquisition through the back door. You may say, "I get it, living my soul's purpose will increase my wealth, so I'll just follow my soul." Beware that this is the ego talking. The ego will take on any system of belief or action that appears likely to produce good results. But whenever you follow your ego—even when it seems to be recommending a fulfilling life—you will never reach your soul or deeper self; you will never discover your true purpose. You can't get there from here.

Instead, choose your purpose fully and choose to live by the dictates of your soul, pure and simple—and riches far beyond money will naturally follow. You will feel filled with life and comforted in knowing that your unique expression is being fully manifested.

It's a Complex Hydraulic System

Our triune model of our inner world is crucial for understanding how to live an authentic life. As we have explored throughout, we are made up of three primary parts: our divinity, our soul, and our ego. Although distinct in that they appear as very different energies, they do not work in isolation from one another. The more you experience your connection to all things, the less gripped you will be by your ego. People who experience an extraordinary sense of divinity rarely feel any need to bow to the altar of ego. Instead, they comfortably live their life as an expression of service. They are much more free to follow their soul's calling, unencumbered by fears of what might happen. The more you connect to and experience the divine, the lighter is your ego's claim to your thoughts and feelings and the more your soul is freed to express itself.

This simple relationship between love and ego came home to me many years ago through a story told to me by a colleague named Lois.

Lois' four-year-old daughter wanted to cut her long flowing hair, never having had it cut before. Lois said no to the request, not wanting to lose her daughter's long locks. Soon the daughter went to the bathroom and, unbeknownst to Lois, cut huge shanks of hair from either side. When Lois saw it, she was horrified and yelled at her daughter, "You cut your hair after I specifically forbade you to."

"No I did not," asserted her daughter, her ego seeking whatever morsels of protection it could find.

"Yes, you did," Lois countered.

"No I didn't," her daughter shot back, unwilling to admit the truth for fear of the consequences.

"Then who did?"

"I don't know," replied her daughter sheepishly, "it just got this way."

The battle continued with Lois in a fury and the child in complete denial, trying desperately to maintain her dignity, until finally Lois' husband came in, having witnessed the tail end of the exchange. He said to the daughter with compassion, "Do you know that no matter what you said or did, we will always love you?"

"Yes," replied the daughter, feeling his love right then and there.

"So tell me," queried the father gently, "how did your hair get this way?"

"I cut it myself, even though Mommy said I shouldn't. I'm sorry."

The more you live consistent with your soul's deepest desire, the more fulfilled your life will be. And the more fulfilled your life is, the less your ego needs to drive you. Ego concerns then recede into the background, because the core from which you are living is so bright that the ego becomes inconsequential. Pierre Teilhard de Chardin spoke of this when he said:

> Some day, after mastering the winds,
>
> the waves, the tides and gravity,
>
> we shall harness for God the energies of Love,
>
> and then, for a second time in
>
> the history of the world,
>
> Humanity will have discovered Fire.

Your soul's purpose is fulfilled only when it is used. Your soul is a great gift—not just to you, but to all of life. In the end, the key to fulfillment is to choose to be used up by life, such that you can say at the end of your time on Earth, "I was used well; I gave my all in service to the world and in service to my soul, and I discovered along the way that both are one and the same." If you can say that, you will have reclaimed your birthright and led a life consistent with the awareness that we are all connected, and that separation is just an illusion.

The goal is not the eradication of the ego. Instead, it is wholeness. If you get nothing else from reading this book, I urge you to consider this. The problem is not the ego, for it has an important place in our inner cosmology. Without it there is no striving, and no drive for achieving our full potential. Rather, the problem is that the ego has taken center stage to the point that our soul and our divinity are lost. When our soul and divinity take their rightful place on the throne of our lives, then our ego also finds its place too, and quietly offers its gifts. The end result is wholeness of the self—a balanced unity of all the parts of us that make up a glorious whole at the center of our being. It is in wholeness—where all parts work synergistically in the service of a full and rich experience of life—that true fulfillment resides. Wholeness does not exclude any part of ourselves, or any part of the world. Instead, all parts are in conscious service to the whole, and we operate from a place of awareness and choice.

An Exercise

Imagine your life as a mythical tale, filled with dragons, fairy godparents, angels, monsters, heroic deeds, maidens in distress, etc. And imagine that your soul has been aching all along to manifest itself in its full glory. Along the way, it was not heard, or if heard, not heeded. But eventually, you did something extraordinary and heard its calling, and from then on your life changed. You embodied yourself.

Now write the story of your life in the spirit of that mythical tale. Consider the obstacles and mighty challenges, and the heroic efforts required and made to overcome the script you were once living. Let it unfold as you write the story. Give yourself permission to have a glorious ending or a glorious future. Let your soul speak to you as you write the story, as if it is writing it for you. Give yourself room to be surprised.

Okay, I Guess You Need a Plan, Sort Of

Now we complete this part of our journey. If you have been diligent, you have followed the exercises in this book and seen your soul's script unfold before you. And hopefully, by now you have chosen to embrace this script, in part or in full.

But the real journey has just begun, for once you find your deeper self, the challenge is to live by it—to follow your inner muse rather than our culture's seeming imperatives. This is the hard part.

I am not enamored with plans when it comes to a soul-driven life. Your soul has a plan but it does not express itself in the ways our ego tends to plan. Throw out your plans filled with Gantt charts, timelines, and key milestones. They are useful for projects, but not when it comes to our soul. In many ways they will snuff out the life force of soul quite rapidly.

Instead, you might want to have a set of guideposts or principles to live your life by. These principles might include some of the following:

- Make decisions from my heart and soul, not from my head.
- Listen to my body, for it knows the way.
- Act with integrity, no matter what.
- Remain deeply curious.

These principles offer guidance that support our soul's unfolding.

Write down each principle on a card and keep it close by. Check these principles often and examine the degree to which you are embodying them. Observe the tension between what you are expressing and what, at the deepest level of your knowing, you are meant to be expressing. And keep moving toward your deepest self.

As you live your life this way, you will find that occasionally fear and unconscious habits still take over. These apparent setbacks are a part of the path as well. If you treat each moment of straying as a learning opportunity, you will come back to the path more easily. And stray you will, for the patterns of your life are deeply etched in your makeup and do not suddenly disappear. To live a full life guided by your inner compass requires that one stay awake moment by moment, knowing that living authentically is a constant choice, now and now and now. It is a path that over time will increasingly feel natural and easy. If you stray, then come back to the path quickly and don't revert to your old and set ways. Instead, follow the guidance of the famous Sufi poet who said:

The breeze at dawn has secrets to tell you;

Don't go back to sleep.

You must ask for what you really want;

Don't go back to sleep.

People are going back and forth across

the doorsill where the two worlds touch.

The door is round and open.

Don't go back to sleep.

NOTES

1. For a powerful treatise on this very subject, see Julian Jaynes (1990), The Origin of Consciousness in the Breakdown of the Bicameral Mind. Houghton Mifflin.

2. http://www.cdc.gov/mentalhealthsurveillance/fact_sheet.html.

3. 2008 NIMH report: The Numbers Count: Mental Disorders in America.

4. Centers for Disease Control and Prevention. (2012). Youth Risk Behavior Surveillance-United States, 2011. Morbidity and Mortality Weekly Report, 61(4).

5. http://www.cdc.gov/mentalhealthsurveillance/fact_sheet.html.

6. http://www.cdc.gov/nchs/fastats/suicide.htm.

7. 2008 NIMH report: The Numbers Count: Mental Disorders in America.

8. Cynthia Ogden, et. al., Center for Disease Control, NCHS Data Brief, no. 82, January 2012, Prevalence of Obesity in the United States, 2009-2010.

9. CDC's Morbidity and Mortality Weekly Report of October 31, 2008.

10. http://www.gallup.com/poll/123887/u.s.-diabetes-rate-climbs-above-11-could-hit-15-2015.aspx.

11. David Riesman, Nathan Glazer, Reuel Denney (2001). The lonely crowd: a study of the changing American character. Yale University Press.

12. Tim Kelley, (2009). True Purpose: 12 strategies for discovering the difference you are meant to make, Berkeley, CA, Transcendent Solutions Press.

13. Antoine De Saint-Exupery, (1943) The Little Prince, Trans. Katherine Woods. New York: Reynal & Hitchcock.

14. New Revised Standard Version (Oxford, 1989).

INDEX

INNER FREEDOM

Dear Keith:

I have finished the book. It is more than I had hoped. As a result of reading the book, I find myself looking at my life and my reactions very differently. The thought of being truly honest in a connected, heartfelt way is both very comforting and invigorating, and at the same time daunting. I always thought of myself as honest. Not even close, from the perspective of this "new Inner Compass framework" you have embraced and shared. I am seeing my life and my world very differently. I find that in almost every situation I am now faced with, I am embracing rather than confronting. I have been experiencing far less anxiety replaced by a calm confidence and patience. The feeling is dramatic. I have always been mistrustful of instant transformation and breakthroughs, but I feel surprisingly grounded.

Your dwelling on how to present your truth in a heartfelt and considered way is very important and powerful. I do not think it can be overstated. I found it to be the most significant and important aspect of the book. I was concerned as I was reading about being compelled to say exactly "your inner truth". I have been very upset with people in my past being outright hurtful under the guise of "just being honest", actually attacking with "you just can't handle my level of honesty". By so doing they absolve themselves of any responsibility or consequences as a result of their cloaked insensitive angry attack. There is a freedom in your "recipe" for delivering the communication. It provides a hopeful confidence that your communication will be received in a productive way and a "nudge" to go ahead and say it.

I am deeply grateful for the gift of this book in my life.

Rob F.

What we are passing on to the next generation is not wisdom from our hearts and souls, but our own sense of loss and fear, and our own lock-step conformity to certain expectations.» So begins Dr. Keith Merron›s book on Inner Freedom: Living Authentically the Life You Were Truly Meant to Live.

Dr. Merron writes using language to convey ideas that are fresh, devoid of cliches, so we are ale to see and understand our lives and legacies differently. It is written with heartfelt insights from a seasoned corporate consultant, managing partner, and teacher.

Dr. Peller Marion, Author of *Career Tune-Up* and
Crisis Proof Your Career

Inner Freedom is an articulate, careful examination into our true nature, one that honors the reader's intelligence and essential whole-ness. Whether Dr. Merron is identifying the difference between ego, soul, and spirit, or guiding us through an exercise in self-inquiry, he stands in a deeply caring place, teaching as one dear friend would teach another – face to face, sharing and celebrating the full spectrum of our humanness, from our darkest shadows to our greatest light. This book should be displayed prominently in every library and in every thera-pist's office, offered to intelligent seekers who need guidance along the path of awakening to true inner freedom.

Lion Goodman, co-author, *Creating on Purpose: The Spiritual Technology of Manifesting Through the Chakras*,
co-founder of Luminary Leadership Institute

When I first began Keith Merron›s Inner Freedom course, I had a notion of the work I felt called to pursue but shied away from claiming it publicly with ease. Keith's guidance worked on me like a river on a stone, gently but powerfully smoothing edges that I hadn't even known were rough. This is the most powerful kind of guide – one who can get into the nooks and crannies we carefully hide from ourselves, not to shame us, but to free us. I am indebted to Keith for helping me take a stand with greater clarity and ease for the work I know is true for me.

Sam Teixeira, Owner, Savvy Young Writers, Menlo Park, CA

Authenticity is a vital issue if we are to live our true purpose and become effective in our world. Keith Merron awakens that impulse with fresh, authentic writing, and a bold plan to regain your integrity. Full of useful information, practical exercises, and inspiring stories, you'll find a living workshop within these pages.

Anodea Judith, author *Eastern Body, Western Mind,*
The Global Heart Awakens

I loved *Inner Freedom*, completely. The balance of content and exercises seems perfect, and you make somewhat complex concepts wonderfully accessible. Keith, you have something truly amazing here and I'm a very, very tough critic when it comes to things like this. I've been reading a lot of books like this lately and I haven't seen anything this good.

Marybeth Tahar, Former Chairman, Interaction Associates,
Founder, Mastery Squared

CPSIA information can be obtained at www.ICGtesting.com
Printed in the USA
BVOW03s0155280414

351336BV00004B/14/P